The Witch of
the Forest's Guide to

FOLKLORE
MAGICK

First published in 2025 by Leaping Hare Press
an imprint of The Quarto Group.
1 Triptych Place 2nd Floor, 185 Park Street
London, United Kingdom
SE1 9SH

T (0)2077 009 000
www.Quarto.com

Text © 2025 Lindsay Squire
Design and illustrations © 2025 Quarto

Lindsay Squire has asserted her moral right to be identified as the Author of this Work in accordance with the Copyright Designs and Patents Act 1988.

All rights reserved. No part of this book may be reproduced or utilized in any form or by any means, electronic or mechanical, including photocopying, recording, or by any information storage and retrieval system, without permission in writing from Leaping Hare Press.

Every effort has been made to trace the copyright holders of material quoted in this book. If application is made in writing to the publisher, any omissions will be included in future editions. A catalog record for this book is available from the British Library.

ISBN: 978-0-7112-9387-8
eBook ISBN: 978-0-7112-9388-5

10 9 8 7 6 5 4 3 2 1

Cover & interior illustrations by Viki Lester of Forensics & Flowers
Design by Georgie Hewitt

Printed in China

The information in this book is for informational purposes only and should not be treated as a substitute for professional counseling, medical advice or any medication or other treatment prescribed by a medical practitioner; always consult a medical professional. Any use of the information in this book is at the reader's discretion and risk. The author and publisher make no representations or warranties with respect to the accuracy, completeness, or fitness for a particular purpose of the contents of this book and exclude all liability to the extent permitted by law for any errors and omissions and for any injury, loss, damage, or expense suffered by anyone arising out of the use, or misuse, of the information in this book, or any failure to take professional medical advice.

The Witch of
the Forest's Guide to

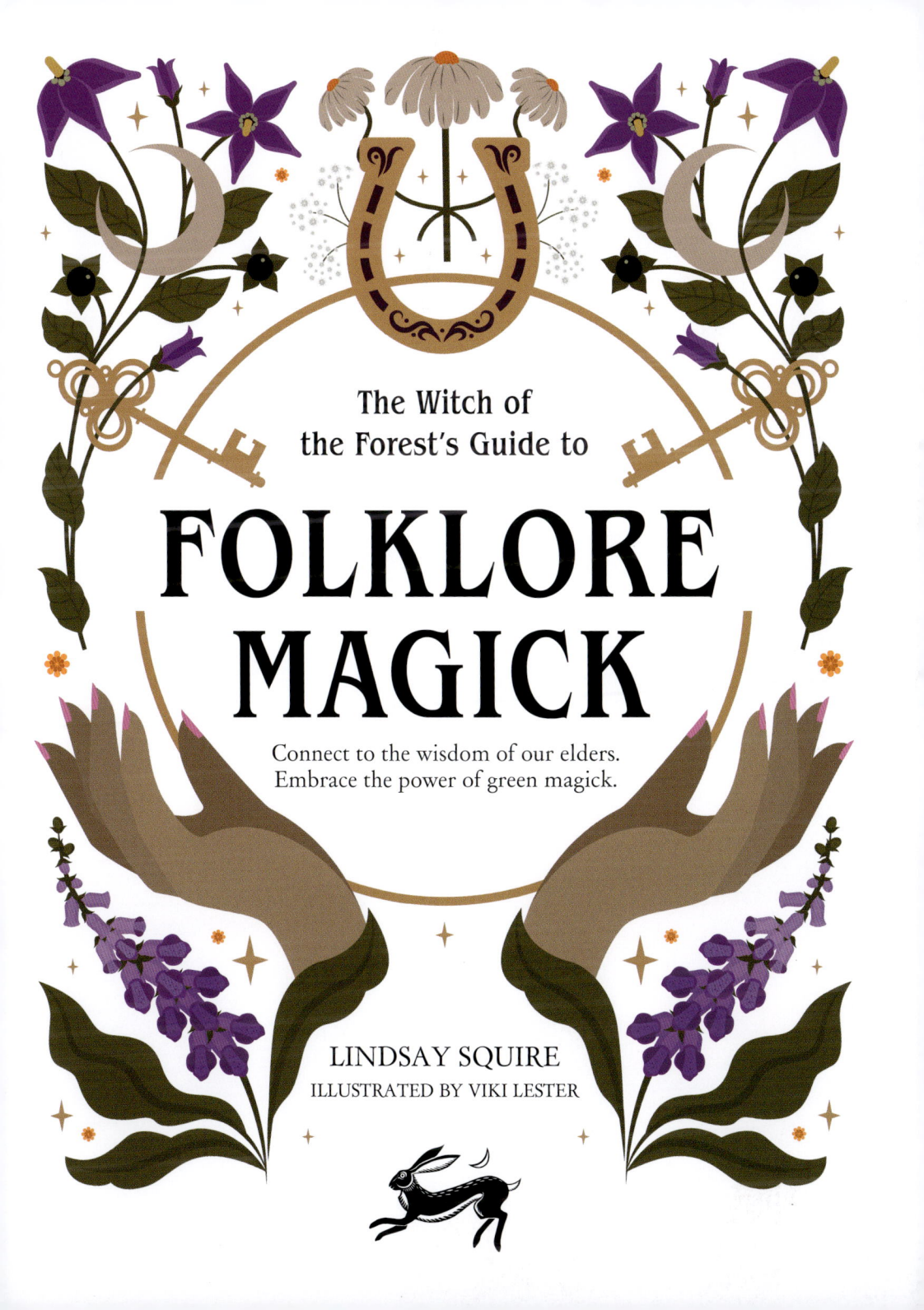

FOLKLORE MAGICK

Connect to the wisdom of our elders.
Embrace the power of green magick.

LINDSAY SQUIRE
ILLUSTRATED BY VIKI LESTER

CONTENTS

INTRODUCTION 6

THINGS TO KNOW BEFORE READING THIS BOOK 9

1. *Practical Folk Herbalism* 10

2. *Herbs & Flowers* 32

3.
Trees 134

4.
Baneful Herbs in Folklore 154

CONCLUSION 170
CITED WORKS 171
FURTHER READING 172
INDEX 173
ACKNOWLEDGMENTS 176

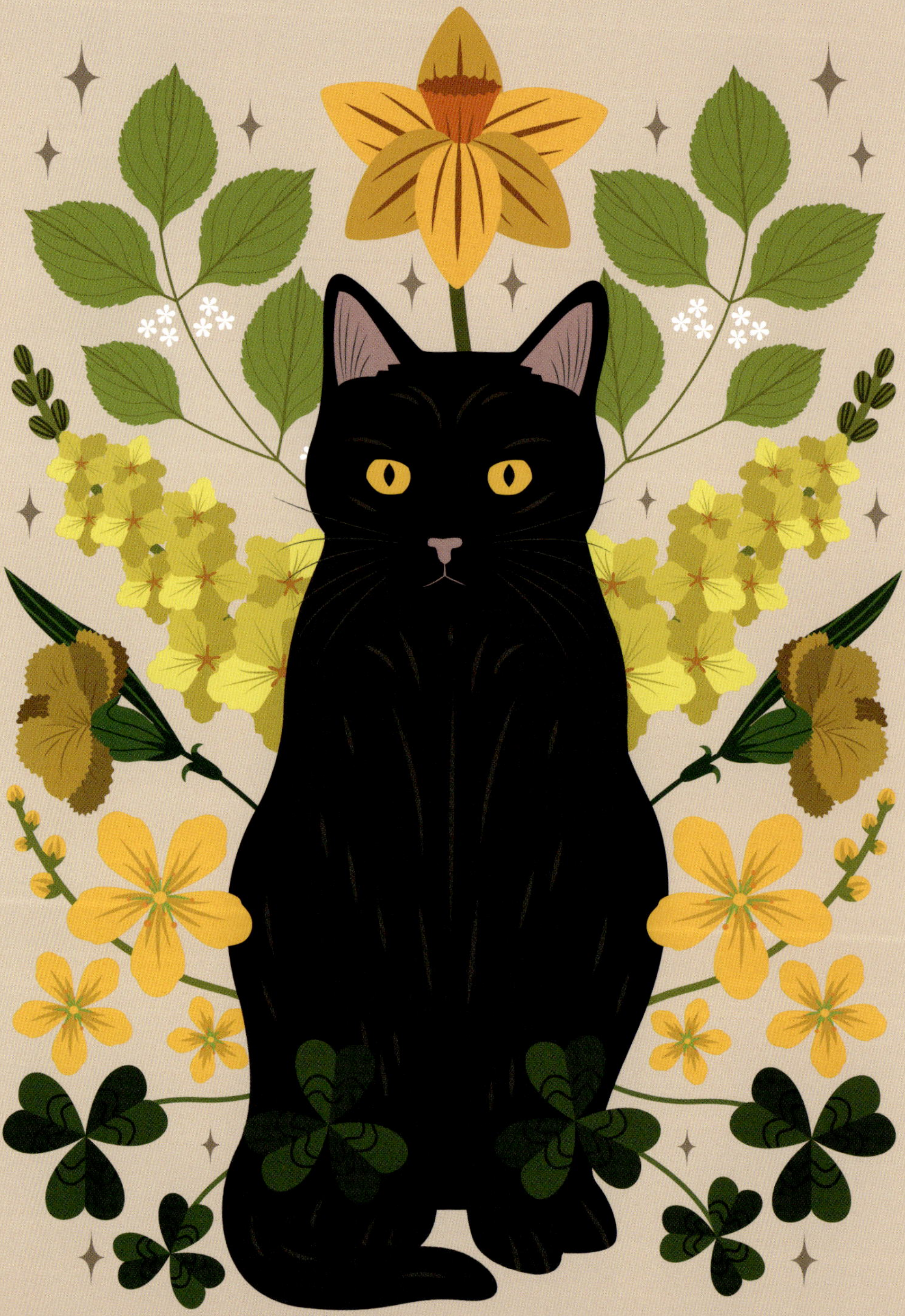

INTRODUCTION

Although I would probably call myself more of an eclectic Witch, as my practice contains elements of all the different kinds of Witchcraft I've practiced over the years, folk magick has, in the last ten years, played an increasingly important role in my Craft. I have never felt drawn to complex spells and rituals using expensive ingredients that are hard to find. I have always valued simplicity in my Craft, where I use what I have available to me both in nature and in places like my home and thrift stores where I can repurpose everyday items for magickal uses. This is essentially what folk magick is all about; it's not meant to be available only to those who can afford it, but is low cost, if not free, and accessible to everyone. This is what I love about folk magick.

I have found myself reading more about not only folk magick, but folklore in general. The word "folklore" is made of two separate words: "folk," which is derived from the German word *volk*, meaning "people," and *lore*, meaning "stories." Folklore is the ancient stories of the people that has its roots in an older way of life. Folklore is a collection of unwritten beliefs, practices, customs, dances, sayings, tales, and traditions that has been passed down through word of mouth from one generation to the next over many centuries.

The German word *volk* (or *folc* in Old English) originally referred to the common people in the lower classes of society, although it later came to mean a group of people in general. One of the many different groups of people (throughout many cultures) who fell into this category were those who practiced Witchcraft. Although it's true that Witches were often solitary wise women, cunning folk, midwives, or the village medicine women who people would visit for cures to all kinds of diseases, there is evidence that, in some cultures and countries (particularly in Europe), many men practiced Witchcraft too, working as healers, which is something that is not generally acknowledged enough. Regardless of gender, they were all healers in their own way and the majority of these Witches came from the lower classes of their communities. These Witches rarely, if ever, committed their medicinal and magickal workings to paper, instead sharing their knowledge verbally to the next generation of Witches and healers.

As common people, folk practitioners like Witches were demonized by the ruling classes of the time, where old age beliefs that were disliked and misunderstood were often attributed to diabolical practices. In this way, Witches were often pushed to the very margins of society. Folk beliefs and practices were also Christianized, where local spirits were turned into saints or other Christian figures, making it even more important that folklore was passed down through the generation in order to preserve the magickal and medicinal knowledge that had been accumulated over the centuries.

Folklore is an important link to our past that helps us to understand and learn about the practices of Witches who have gone before, and to walk the path that our ancestors walked before us. Learning about folklore is to build a very special relationship with the natural world around us and understand nature's healing and magickal powers as they once did. Folklore enables us to teach and preserve the practice, knowledge, and traditions of Witchcraft so they are not lost to the passing of time. It can also help to draw us closer to the natural world around us and enrich our own Witchcraft practice today.

Herbs, flowers, and trees played a huge part in the practice of Witchcraft over the centuries, just as they do today, and they have rich and ancient folklore associated with them. This is the inspiration for this book: the amazing folklore of these natural offerings as well as their folk magick and medicinal uses. The herbs, flowers, and trees found here have all been specifically chosen because they are common to many countries around the world and are easily foraged for (or inexpensive to buy).

I really hope the folklore in this book will help to inspire and enrich your own Craft by bringing you closer to the incredible medicinal and magickal powers of nature to empower your own well-being and healing practices.

Much love,
Lindsay x

THINGS TO KNOW BEFORE *Reading This Book*

What is folklore?
Folklore refers to stories, beliefs, traditions, and myths from a specific group of people of culture that have been passed down through the generations by word of mouth rather than written down. One example of this is the association of the horseshoe with look and good fortune. Legend has it that it was found to be a lucky symbol when a blacksmith nailed a horseshoe to the Devil's cloven hoof. It caused the Devil a great deal of pain and from that point he agreed never to cross the threshold of a house with a horseshoe above the door.

What is green folklore?
Green folklore, the focus of this book, is the stories and legends associated with herbs, flowers, and trees, from many different cultures, that have been passed down by word of mouth.

How can folklore enrich my Craft today?
By learning about the folk stories associated with the herbs, flowers, and trees in this book, you will understand more about their magickal and medicinal properties on a deeper level. Folk stories help you understand not only where herbs come from, but also what they were used for, which will help to enrich your own personal Witchcraft practices.

What is folklore magick?
It is the magickal spells and rituals that have been passed down throughout the centuries. In the context of this book, it is the way cultures such as the ancient Greeks, Egyptians, and Romans, as well as the Celts and magickal practitioners from eastern Europe use herbs, spices, and flowers in spells. Being familiar with herbal folklore not only gives you a wealth of knowledge about how to used herbs, spices, flowers, and trees in your magickal spells and rituals, but it also teaches you how to use these ingredients for healing. Many of our modern-day medicines originate from the natural world (such as willow bark in aspirin), so knowing about the medicinal properties of herbs helps put the power of natural healing into your own hands.

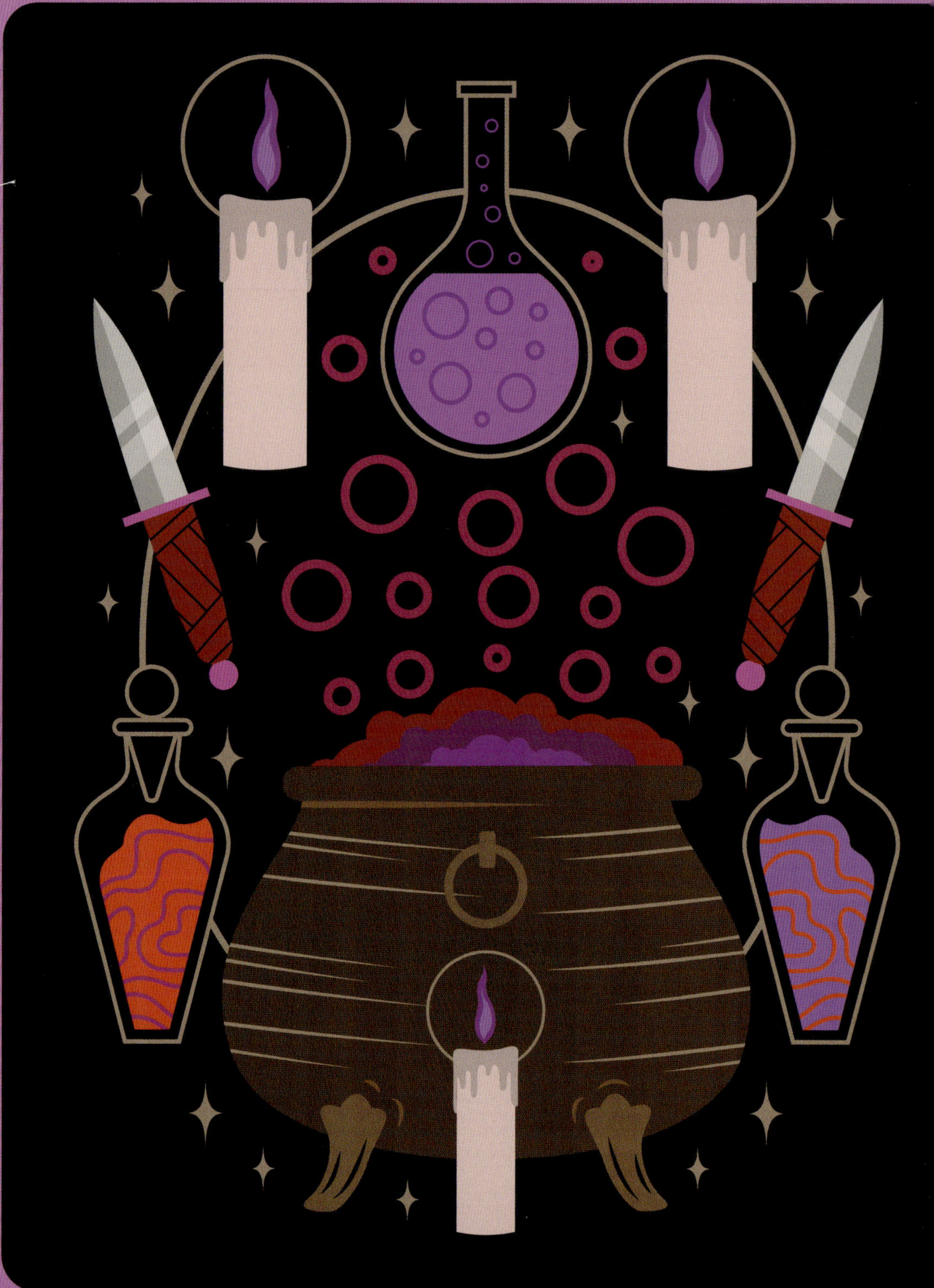

1
PRACTICAL FOLK HERBALISM

Before you delve into the folklore associated with the herbs, spices, flowers, and trees in this book, this chapter will outline the different ways in which these natural ingredients can be used in your Craft.

In chapters two and three, you'll find reference to different kinds of herbal preparations that can be used for both magickal and medicinal purposes. In this chapter, you'll find a description of what each of these preparations are as well as how to make them. I'll be outlining the methods I personally use to make each one, but there are many other methods available, so use one that feels right to you and your practice.

TEA

Tea is a caffeinated drink that is made from the *Camellia sinenis* plant including white, green, and black tea. Herbal tea, however, is non-caffeinated and made from herbs, roots, or stems. Teas are probably the most popular way to use herbs for both magickal and medicinal purposes. Enjoying a cup of herbal tea can be a meditative experience as well as an easy way to introduce herbs into your daily routine. You can make your own blends using loose herbs or the contents of herbal tea bags. Any loose herbal matter left in the bottom of your cup can also be used for tasseoancy (tea leaf reading).

The easiest way to make a cup of tea is to use a tea ball infuser, which can be bought cheaply online. It's best to use dried herbs, spices, or flowers that are cut down so they can easily fit inside the infuser. Store your tea herbs in a jar in a cool, dark place as this will make their medicinal and magickal properties more potent.

Place your chosen herbal blend into the tea ball infuser, then place the infuser into a cup of hot (but not boiling) water, leaving it to steep for 5–10 minutes before drinking. Delicate herbs such as basil and cilantro leaves will only need around 5–7 minutes to steep whereas more robust herbs such as rosemary, thyme, and sage will need a little longer.

If you're not drinking it straight away, your tea can be left to cool and then stored in the refrigerator for up to 3 days.

INFUSION

All teas are technically infusions, but an infusion is made from a larger amount of plant matter (herbs, fruits, roots, and leaves) than a cup of herbal tea. Another significant difference is that plant material in an infusion is left to steep in the hot water for a longer time than a tea. Whereas teas are left to brew for up to 10 minutes, infusions are left to steep for anything from 30 minutes to a couple of hours, which produces a stronger tasting, more potent drink.

To make an infusion, place at least double the amount of plant matter than you would use to make a cup of tea in a jar or teapot and fill with hot (but not boiling) water. Leave to steep for at least an hour (but no more than 2 hours). After this time, drain out the herbs and discard them, and your infusion is ready to drink.

Infusions can also be used magickally for other purposes. Depending on the herbal blend you've chosen, they can be used to wash floors and to wipe down furniture, walls, doors, and mirrors. They can also be poured into your bath water as part of a ritual bath. Store infusions in the refrigerator for up to 3 days if you're not using or drinking them straight away.

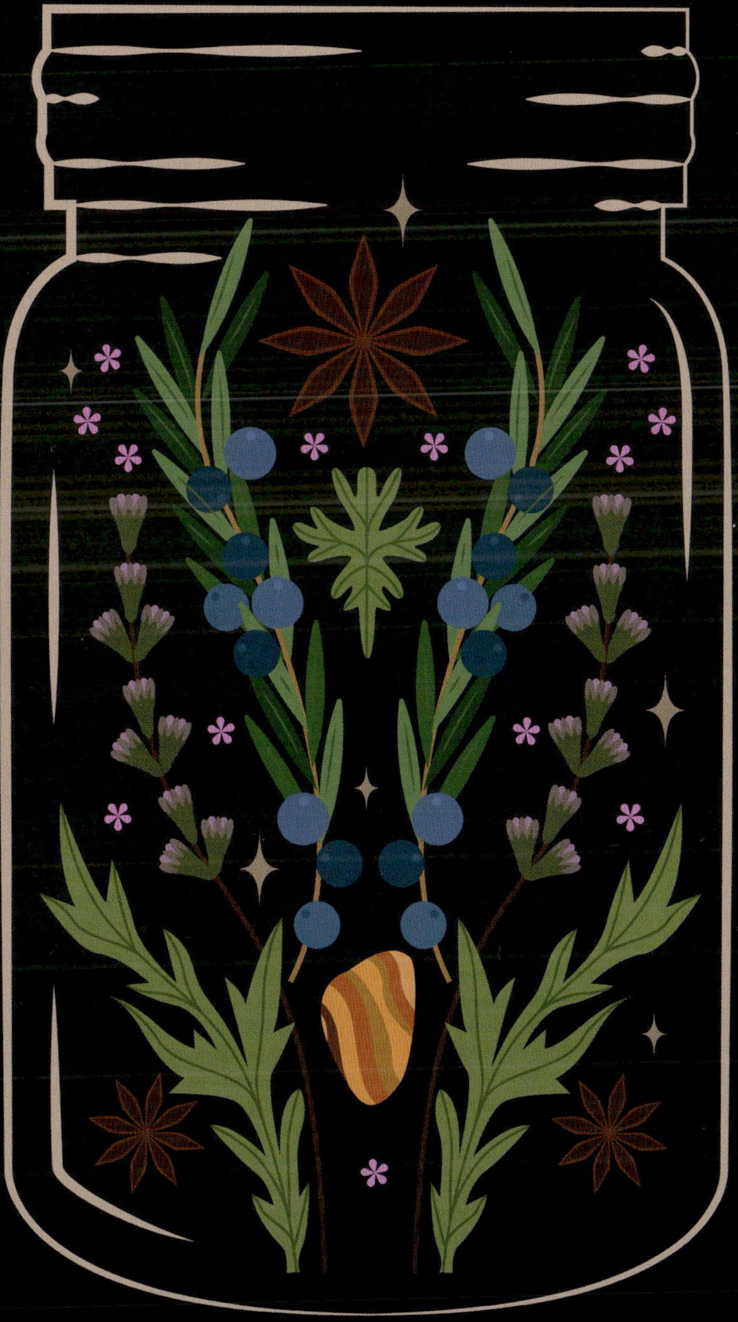

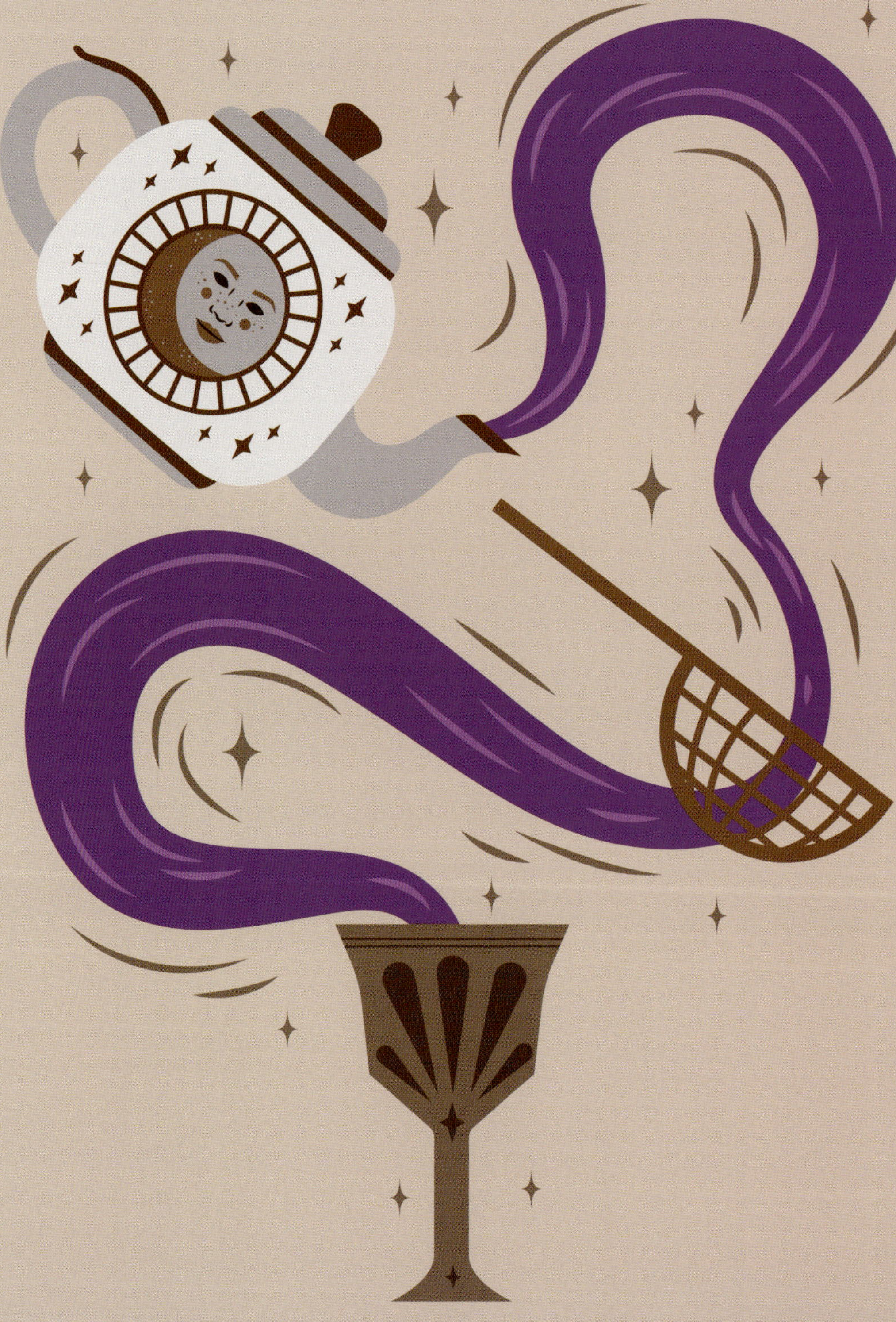

TISANE

A tisane is a more potent type of herbal tea that is left to steep for much longer than your average tea. Tisanes are made by soaking herbs in hot water to bring out their magickal and medicinal properties in much the same way as teas and infusions. However, they are steeped for several hours or days. The most famous tisane is chamomile. It is made only with aromatic chamomile flowers and is completely caffeine free, making it a popular tisane for Witches in centuries past and today.

To make a tisane, place the herbs, spices, and flowers of your choice into a glass jar containing hot (but not boiling water), and leave to steep from 4 hours up to a few days in a cool, dark place. Once ready, drain out the herbal matter through a tea strainer, sieve, or cheesecloth, and then it's ready to drink. Store in the refrigerator for 2–3 days if you're not drinking it straight away.

OIL

Oils are another popular way to use herbs for medicinal and magickal purposes. They are best used externally and can be rubbed onto stings and bites or incorporated into spell work by anointing yourself and your ritual tools, and dressing candles. In the 19th century, the Irish Witch Biddy Early often used herbal oils in her healing practices, using them to cure local people and even their animals, who came to her with all kinds of afflictions.

To make an oil, first choose a carrier oil such as grapeseed, almond, or olive oil. Take your chosen herbs, plants, spices, or flowers, in either dried or fresh form, and chop them up into small pieces. Place the plant matter into an airtight jar and then fill with your carrier oil.

Once filled, secure the lid and store in a cool, dark place, shaking the bottle regularly. Leave to infuse for 4 weeks, then drain out the plant matter. Your oil is then ready to use.

Alternatively, to make a more potent oil, once you have drained out the herbs, add another batch of herbs to the drained oil in the same quantities as you did before, and leave to infuse for another 4 weeks, shaking daily. After this time, drain and discard the plant matter. If you want to make a super concentrated oil, repeat the process for a third time, leaving it for another month before using. Once made, a herbal oil can keep for up to 6 months if stored in a cool, dark place.

The exact amount of oil and herbs to use are given in this book for each recipe, but if you are unsure as to how much to use when creating your own recipes, a good starting point is to use three times as much oil to the amount of herbs in the jar.

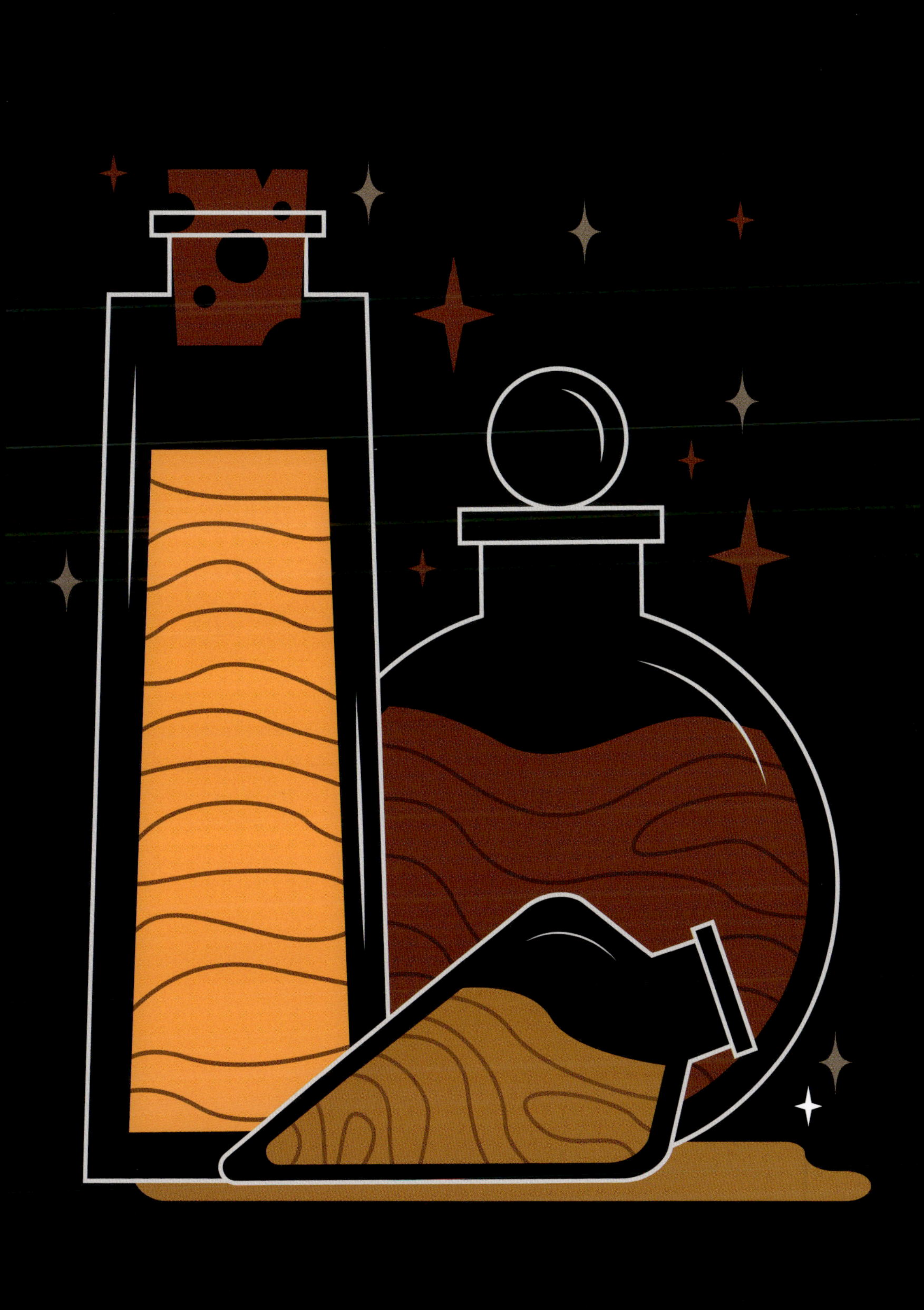

TINCTURE

A tincture is made in much the same way as an oil, but uses alcohol instead of a carrier oil. Unlike oils, tinctures are usually taken internally and can be dropped from a dropper bottle under the tongue or added to food or drink. A general daily dose of a tincture can range from 20 to 60 drops, but is usually spread out into three measures throughout the day.

To make a tincture, fill an airtight jar with your chosen herbs, then fill the rest of the jar with 80–100 proof alcohol. Vodka is a good choice as it is not only strong enough in terms of alcohol content, but it doesn't have a great deal of flavor on its own, so the herbs you use will be more prominent in terms of taste. A rough rule is to use one part herbs and five parts alcohol, but for the herbs, spices, and flowers in this book where a tincture recipe is included, the exact amounts of herbs and alcohol are given. For a basic tincture though 4 oz (110 g) of herbs will require 20 fl oz (600 ml) of alcohol.

Store the jar in a cool, dark place, leaving the alcohol and herbs to infuse for a minimum of 4 weeks (but no longer than 6 weeks), shaking regularly during this time. The longer you leave your tincture to infuse, the more concentrated it will become. After this time, strain out the herbal mixture into a bowl using a cheesecloth, squeezing out as much liquid as possible. Pour the alcohol into a dark bottle, labeling it with the date. Store the bottle out of direct sunlight.

As alcohol is a preservative, your tincture will keep for at least 1 year, and some will last for several years.

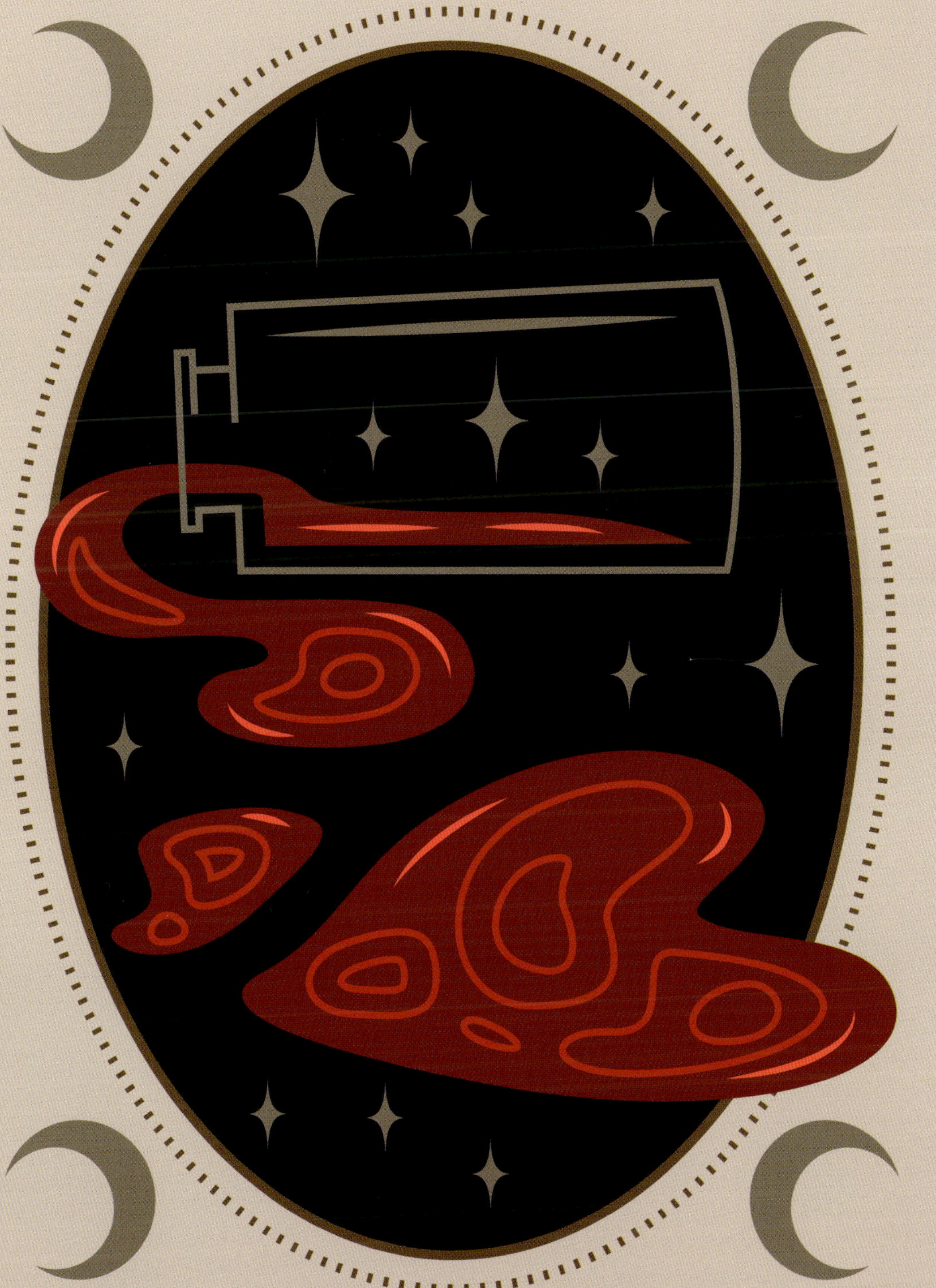

SALVE

Herbal salves (also known as balms or ointments) are simple to make and are rubbed onto the body to soothe skin conditions or relieve muscle pain. Salves are similar to balms, although balms are a little firmer. They are sometimes called ointments, and one of the most famous ointments within the practice of Witchcraft is the flying ointment. In times past, Witches would rub this hallucinogenic ointment, made from psychotropic herbs such as belladonna and foxglove, over their bodies in order to aid astral travel to Sabbats.

To make a salve, you need to first make a herbal oil for the base (see page 18). Choose the herbs, plants, and flowers that match the magickal or medicinal purpose you want to use it for (see chapter 2 for ideas). If you don't have a herbal oil, you can use a plain carrier oil such as grapeseed, or jojoba.

A basic salve recipe uses 8 fl oz (235 ml) of oil (plain or infused) to 1 oz (30 g) of beeswax. If your oil is plain, you can use up to 50 drops of essential oils of your chosen medicinal herbs, but it's important to research the essential oil you wish to use, as not all essential oils are skin safe. Different oil blends also require different ratios of essential oil to carrier oil in order to safely dilute them before applying to the skin.

Place the beeswax and infused or plain oil in a double boiler (or in a heat-proof bowl placed over a pan of water) on a low heat, stirring until they have completely melted. Once melted, remove the bowl from the heat and add any essential oils, stirring well. While the mixture is still hot, pour the liquid into an airtight jar and leave to cool. Leave the salve overnight to fully harden, and then it's ready to use. Store in a cool, dark place. Herbal salves last up to a year.

To create a firm balm, a general ratio of beeswax to oil is 1:3
To make a semisolid salve, a general ratio of beeswax to oil is 1:4
To create a very soft salve, a general ratio of beeswax to oil is 1:5

SALVE

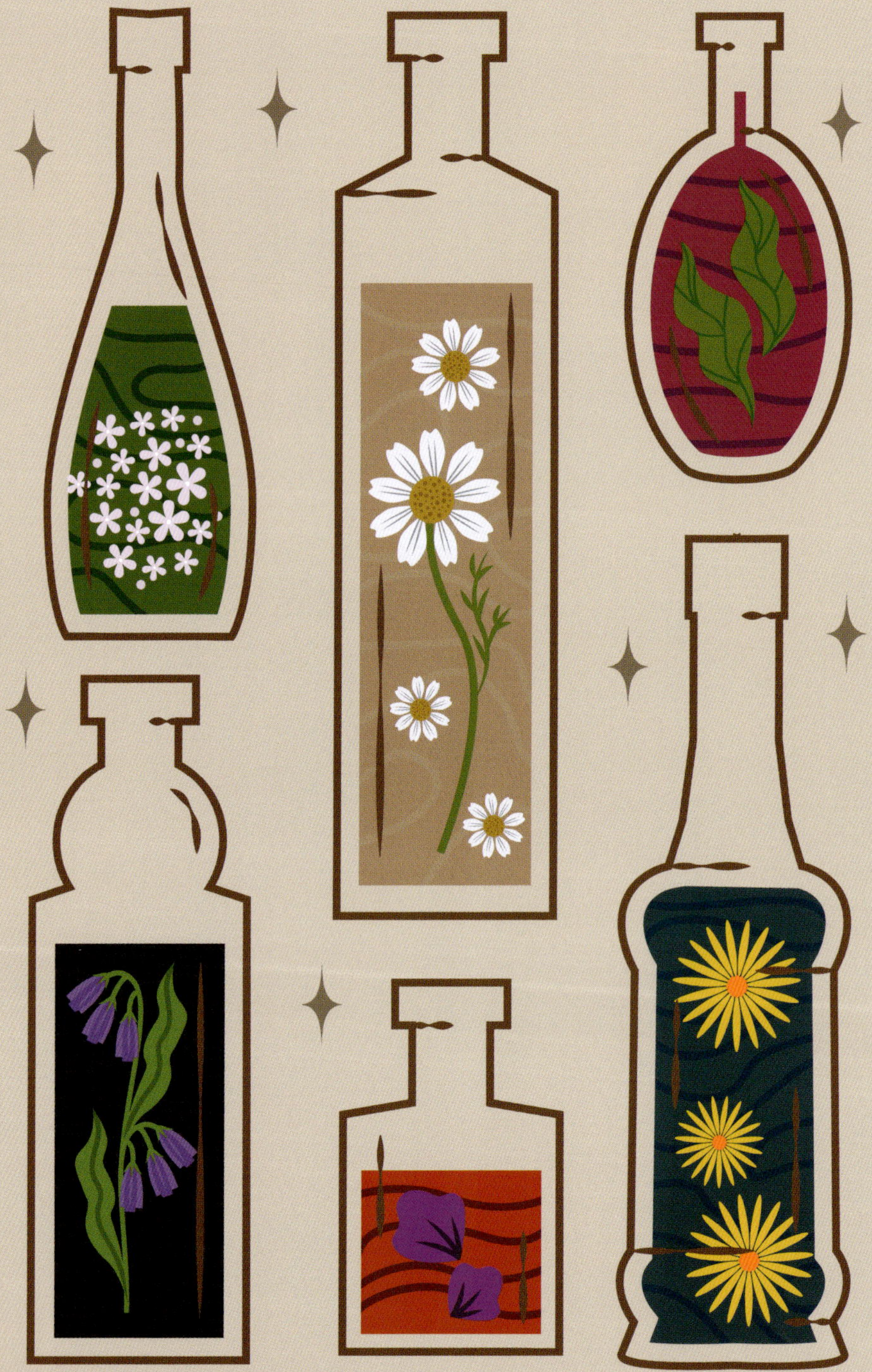

LINIMENT

A liniment is a topical remedy that is rubbed onto the body to help relieve pain and stiffness in muscles and soft tissues. Rubbing alcohol and witch hazel are often used for the base of a liniment (along with herbs of your choice), as they are quickly absorbed by the skin, taking the goodness of the herbs into the body with them. Oil can also be used as a base but the effect isn't as immediate as a liniment made with alcohol or witch hazel.

Good herbs to use in a liniment include comfrey, arnica, willow bark, yarrow, and chamomile as they all help to calm inflammation and reduce pain. A famous liniment called A.B.C Liniment was sold in the late 19th century, and three of its primary ingredients were belladonna, aconite, and chloroform, all highly dangerous herbs and substances. It is not surprising that there were many instances of poisoning from using this liniment!

To make a liniment, add 1–2 tbsp of your chosen herbs (dried or fresh) into a clean airtight jar. Next, pour in enough witch hazel, rubbing alcohol, or vodka into the jar to cover the herbs, then leave to steep in a cool dry place for 4–6 weeks, shaking daily. After this time, strain out the herbs using a cheesecloth, squeezing out as much liquid as possible and return the liquid to the bottle. If you are adding any essential oils, do so now. Your liniment is now ready to use. Shake the bottle before each use.

Since alcohol and witch hazel are both preservatives, your liniment will keep for a good few years if stored in a cool, dark place.

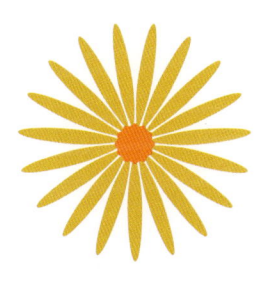

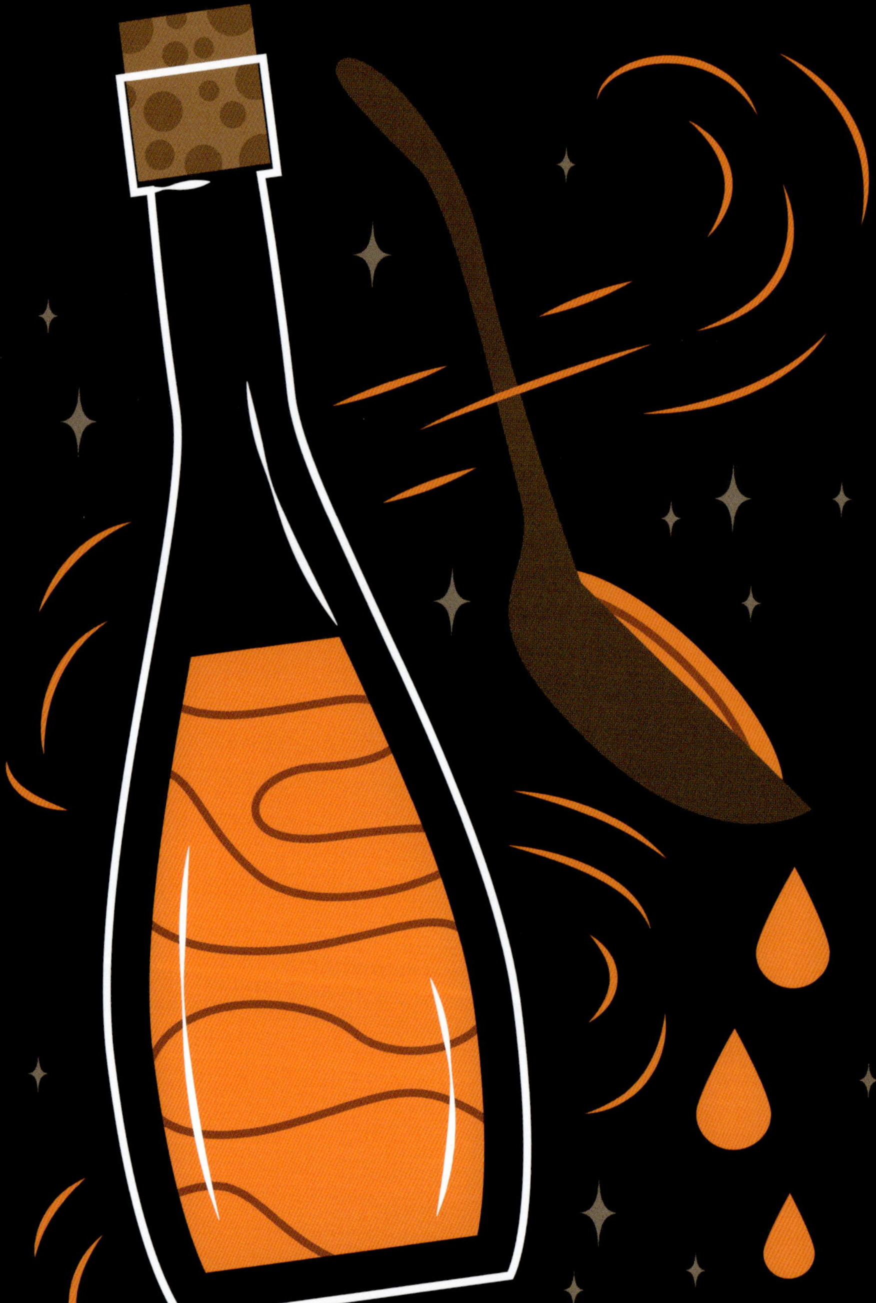

SYRUP

Syrups are sweetened infusions or decoctions preserved with sugar or honey, and are used to relieve sore throats and soothe coughs. The sweetness of the syrup helps to disguise any unpleasant taste that may be present due to the different plant matter used.

The base for a syrup is a decoction, which is a simmered tea made from dried berries, roots, seeds, or tree bark that is similar to a herbal infusion, but much more concentrated. To make a syrup, chop up the plant material you have chosen and add enough water to cover it. Simmer on low heat for 30–45 minutes. Remove the pan from the stovetop and drain and discard the herbs using a sieve. At this point you can add 2 tbsp of more delicate herbs like basil, dill, cilantro, or any flowers that are too fragile to be boiled for so long. Return the pan of infused water and herbs to the stovetop and simmer for another 10–15 minutes on a low heat. After this time, drain and discard the herbs and add an equal amount of honey to the amount of infused water left in the pan. Heat the mixture for a further 5–10 minutes until the syrup thickens before pouring it into an airtight jar. Once cooled, it's ready to use and will keep for about a month. This syrup will keep for about 3 months.

One of the most famous syrups used by healers, wise women, Witches and non-Witches alike is elderberry syrup. It is used as a powerful cold preventative and remedy because one cup of elderberries contains nearly 60% of the recommended daily allowance of vitamin C, making it a powerful source of antioxidants.

POULTICE

A poultice is used to apply herbs in paste form directly onto the skin, and can be used to treat aches, pains, minor wounds, bug bites, rashes, and inflammation. Good herbs to use for this purpose include lemongrass, ginger, turmeric, and camphor.

There are many ways to make a poultice. An easy method is to cut up your chosen herbs (fresh or dried), place them into a muslin or linen bag, and then soak in hot water for 5 minutes. Take the bag out of the water. Knead the herbs through the bag using a rolling pin to break them down before placing them back into the hot water for another 5 minutes, or until the herbs have completely softened. After this time, the poultice is ready to use, and the herbs in the bag can be applied to the affected area. Leave on for 10–15 minutes. Poultices can be applied while warm or after they have cooled, it depends what you are using it for. Warm poultices increase blood flow to the area to treat bruises and abscesses while cold poultices bring relief to sunburn and insect bites and reduce inflammation.

A more traditional way to make a poultice is to grind down a few tablespoons of each of your chosen herbs using a mortar and pestle or food processor and add a little hot water, enough to turn the mixture into a thick paste. Smooth the herbal paste directly onto the skin and leave for 10–15 minutes. Refrigerate the paste and it will keep for up to three days.

Poultices were one of the many methods that wise women in early modern Europe used for healing. Witches such as Barbe Barbier in France in 1613 used poultices, as well as infusions, syrups, and teas to cure those who called upon her to treat a range of different illnesses and diseases.

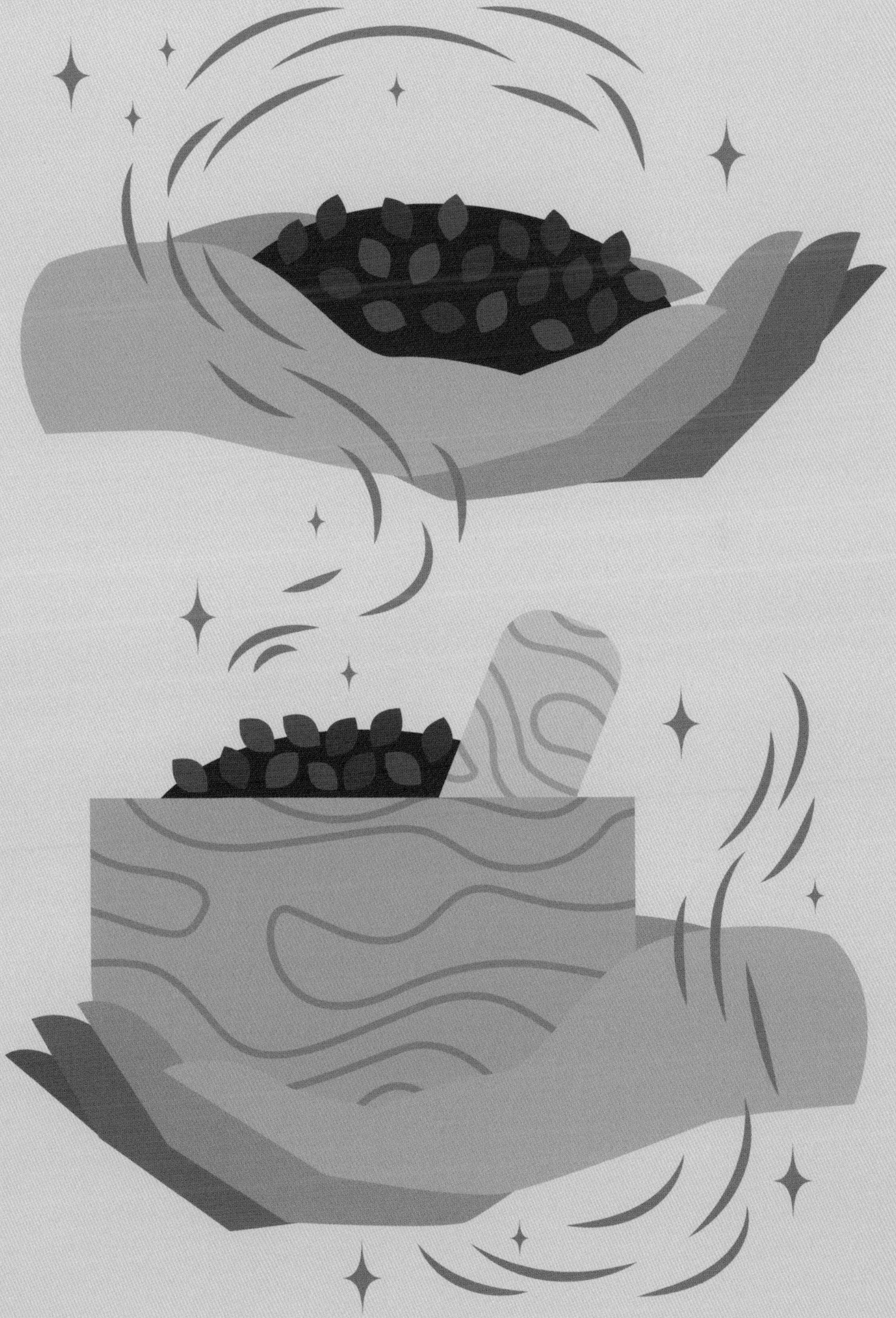

COMPRESS

Like a poultice, a compress is applied directly to the skin, but instead of placing herbs directly onto the affected area, a piece of cloth is soaked in a premade herbal solution before laying it on the body. Hot compresses are best used to relieve muscular aches and pains and help to boost circulation and stimulate the lymphatic system. While cold compresses constrict blood vessels and are good for treating hot conditions like fevers, headaches, swelling, and inflammation.

A traditional way to make a compress is to put a tisane, infusion, or decoction, made from the herbs of your choice, in a bowl, and soak a clean cloth in the solution. You can either warm up the solution by simmering it on a low heat, or it can be used cold from the refrigerator. Ice cubes can also be added to the bowl to make the compress even colder.

Soak the cloth for 10 minutes then squeeze out the excess water and lay it on the affected area, leaving for up to 20 minutes.

You can also make a quick compress using herbal tea bags. Place 3–5 teabags of your choice in a bowl of hot water and leave to steep for 20 minutes, then soak a cloth in the water for a further 10 minutes. After this time, place the cloth on the affected area and leave for up to 20 minutes before removing. Refrigerate the infused water and it will keep for about 3 days.

Agnes Sampson, the 16th-century Scottish healer known as the "Wise Wife of Keith", would use traditional healing methods such as compresses, poultices, and infusions to cure the local people who called upon her for her healing gifts and knowledge. Unfortunately, things didn't end well for Agnes, and she was charged and executed for Witchcraft in January 1591.

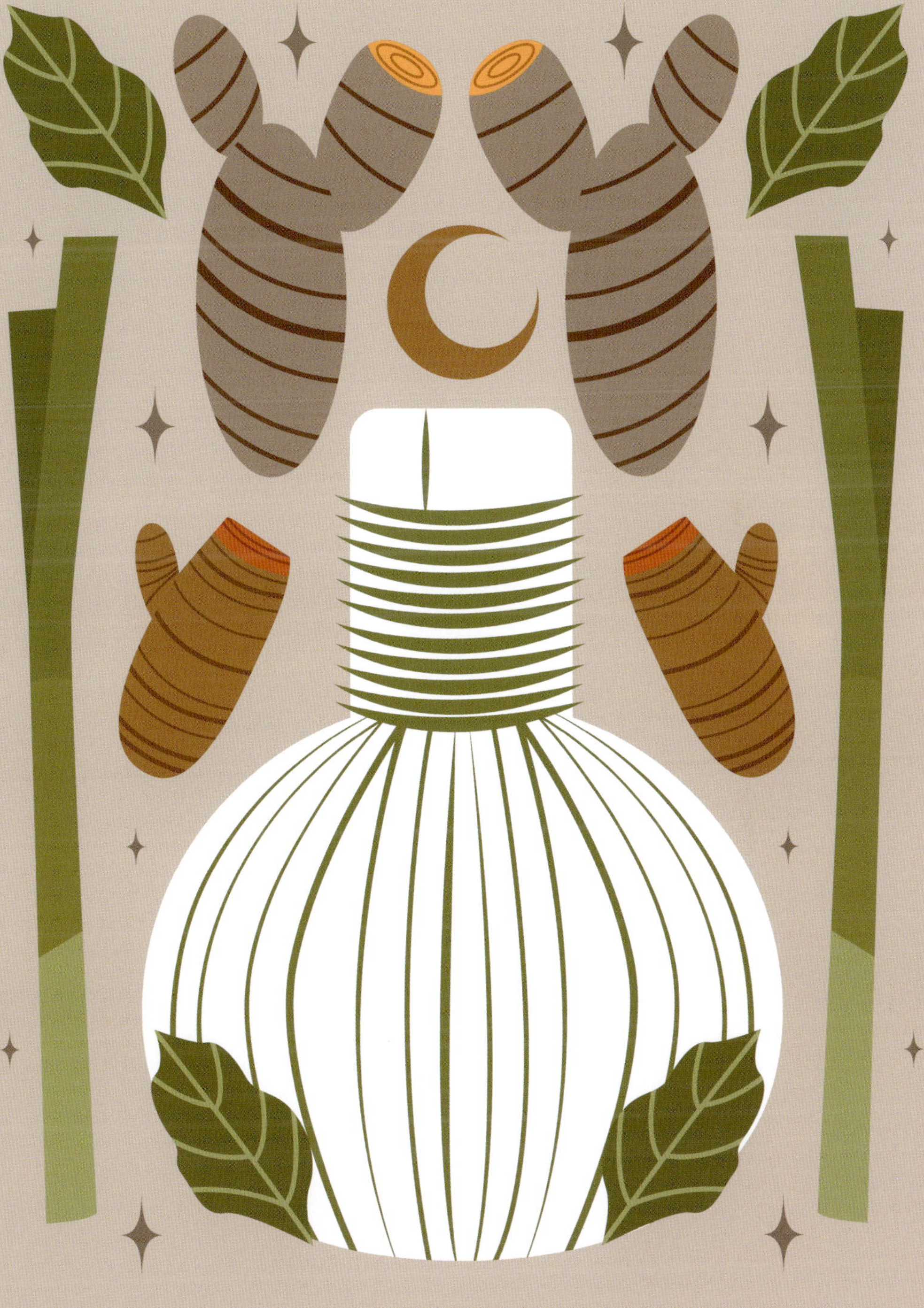

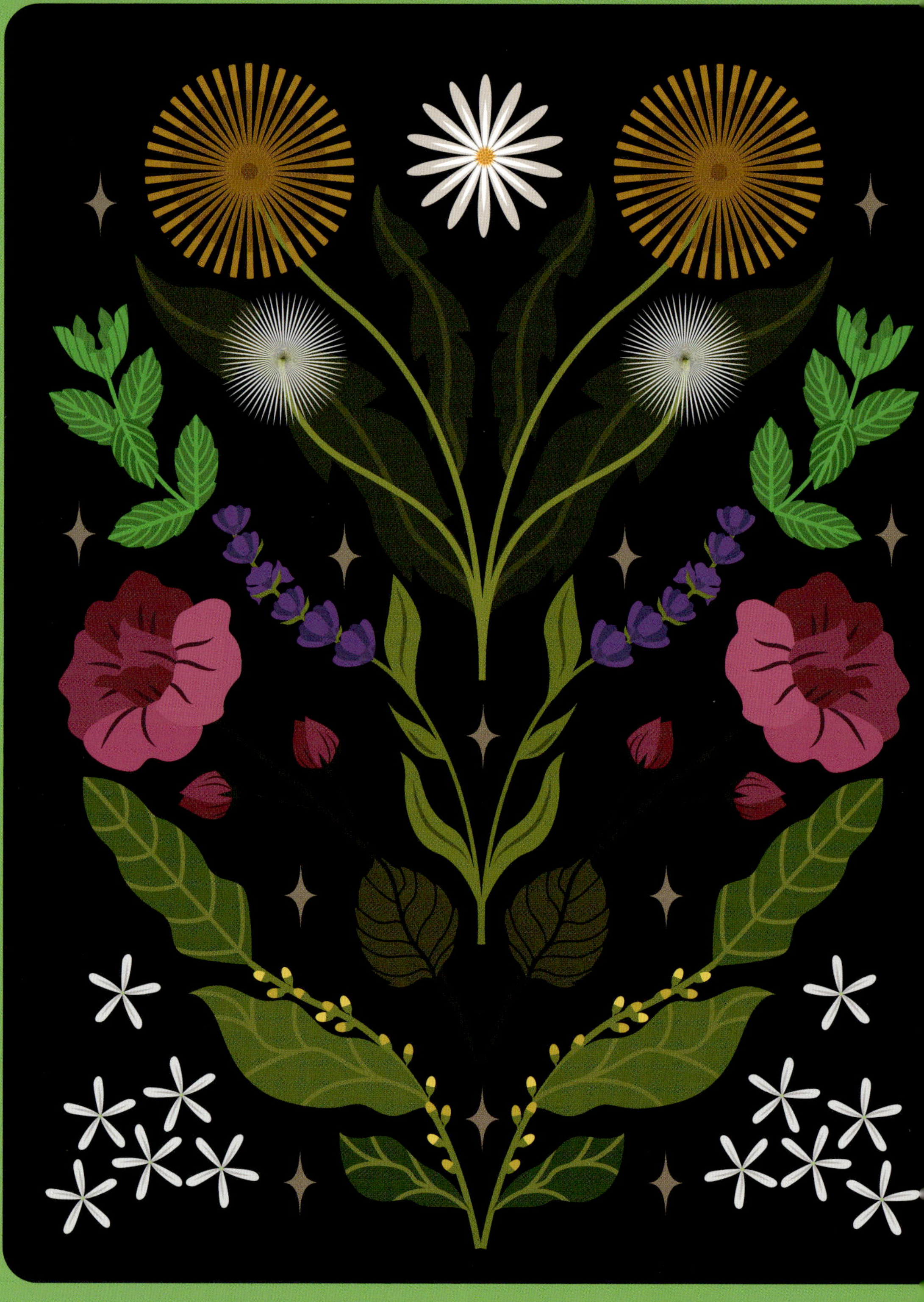

2
HERBS & FLOWERS

Over the thousands of years of human existence, herbs, flowers, and trees have played a large role in our everyday lives, whether that has been in what we eat, what we use to build the places we live in, or in the making of medicines for healing. They have and also continue to play a central role in the practice of Witchcraft.

The next two chapters will focus upon the rich and colorful folklore that is associated with many common herbs, flowers, and trees that have been passed down throughout the years from one generation to another. I will also include simple ways to use them in your magickal workings (including modern and old folkloric spells and charms) and, in the tradition of the cunning folk and wise women and men of the past, will also include their medicinal properties and how to use them in your own healing practices.

DISCLAIMER:
This book is written for reference and educational purposes only and is not intended to replace professional medical advice. Please seek the advice of a medical professional before using any of the plants in this book as a form of medicine, especially if you are pregnant or suffer with allergies. If you have any illnesses, consult a medical practitioner before using any remedies in this book.

Herbs

AGRIMONY
Agrimonia eupatoria

FOLKLORE

There are around 15 species of agrimony, each located in different areas of the world. It is a herb with spikes of five-petaled yellow flowers that grows up to 24 in (60 cm) tall, and is found in Europe, north Africa, southwest Asia, and North America. When looking to forage for agrimony, it can most commonly be found in grasslands and hedgerows, and on the edges of fields and roadsides. Both the flowers and the leaves can be used for their medicinal and magickal purposes.

According to folklore, agrimony's Latin name *Agrimonia eupatoria* refers to the king of Pontus, Mithradates VI Eupator (132–63 BC), who was well known for his herbal medicines, wisdom, and knowledge. Agrimony is also known by many other different folk names such as sticklewort and cockelbur due to its burrs or hooked bristles that stick to the fur of animals that brush up against it. It is sometimes also known as church steeples because of how its spikes stand: tall, straight, and proud toward the sky.

MAGICKAL PROPERTIES

Agrimony is primarily associated with sleep. An Old English 11th-century poem stated that "If it be leyd under mann's heed, he shal sleepyn as if he were deed; he shal never drede ne wakyn, till fro under his heed it be takyn." To harness its sleep powers, agrimony can be made into a sleep pillow. Fill a pouch with dried agrimony along with equal parts of lavender, hops, valerian, and chamomile and place under your pillow at night to aid restful sleep. It can also be consumed as a tea (with or without the aforementioned herbs) before bedtime for this purpose. Agrimony

ZODIAC SIGNS
Cancer and Sagittarius

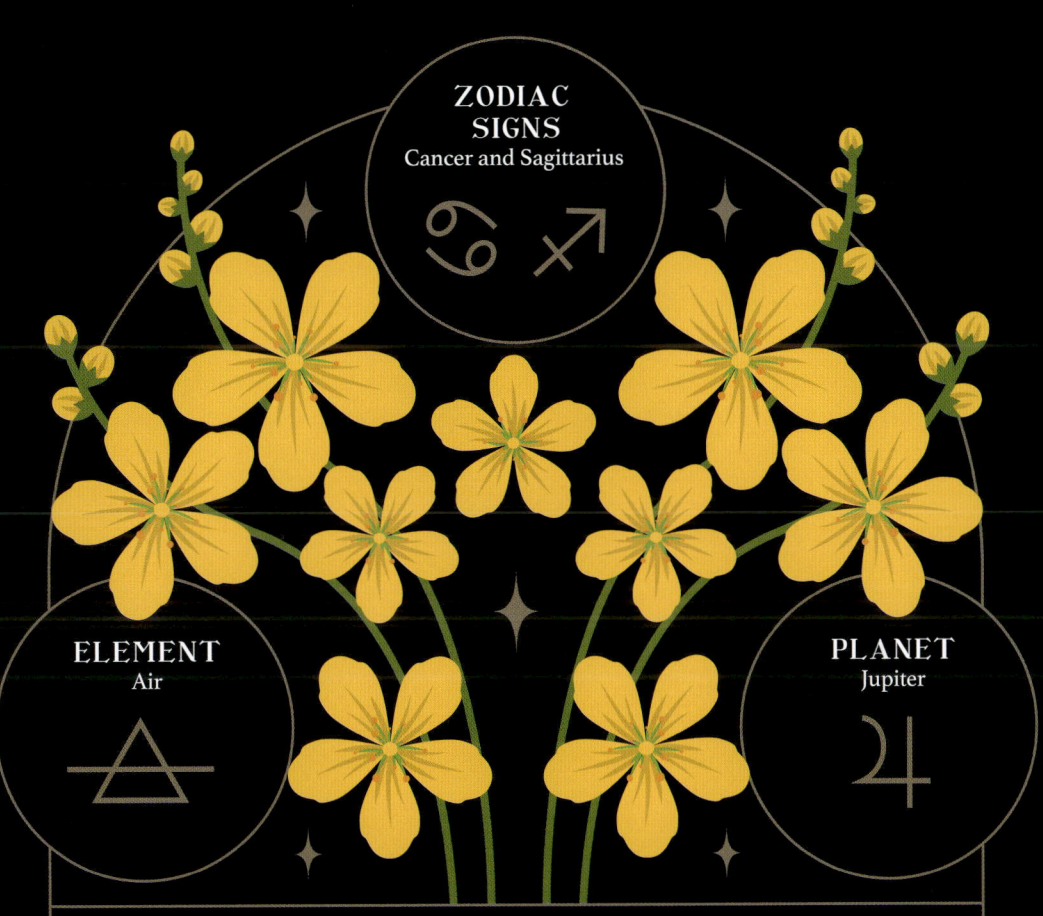

ELEMENT
Air

PLANET
Jupiter

AGRIMONY
Agrimonia eupatoria

MAGICKAL PROPERTIES
- Encourages divinatory dreams
- Enhances psychic abilities
- Offers protection
- Banishes negativity
- Breaks hexes
- Reverses spells
- Cleanses the aura

MEDICINAL PROPERTIES
- Promotes restful sleep
- Soothes sore eyes
- Brightens the skin
- Heals wounds
- Treats snake bites
- Eases diarrhea
- Soothes sore throats
- Eases aching joints
- Cleanses the liver

FOLK NAMES Acrimony, Ackerkraut, Agrimonia, Aigremoine, Burr Marigold, Carclive, Church Steeples, Cocklebur, Common Agrimony, Fairy's Wand, Funffing, Harvest Lice, Liverwort, Odermennig, Stickwort, Sticklewort

dream pillows can also be used in order to promote divinatory dreams. Simply fill a pillow with equal amounts of agrimony, mugwort, vervain, and blue lotus to help you tap into your psychic abilities as you dream.

Agrimony is also known for its protective qualities. Place agrimony, sea salt, and rosemary into a bucket of water and use it to wash your floors to purify your home and keep it protected from ill will or any negative and harmful energies.

Agrimony can also be used as food or offerings for familiar spirits, and is a potent herb to use if you want to break a hex or return any kind of negative energy back to its sender. On a piece of paper, place the name of the person you want to return the hex or unwanted energy back to. Over the name, anoint the paper with agrimony oil as you visualize that energy leaving you and going back to them. Fold the paper away from you three times to symbolize removal and then burn it in a cauldron (a folkloric symbol of manifestation). To make the agrimony oil, add 3 tsp of dried agrimony to 5 fl oz (150 ml) of grapeseed, olive, sunflower, or almond oil and leave in a cool place to infuse for 2 weeks. After this time, drain the herbs and add another 3 tsp of dried agrimony, leaving for another 2 weeks. Drain the herbs, and then your oil is ready to use.

MEDICINAL PROPERTIES

Derived from the Greek word *argemone*, meaning "that which heals the eye," agrimony was used to treat eye maladies. To make eyes bright, the Egyptians, Greeks, and Anglo-Saxons would actually crush agrimony down, collect the sap, and dilute it in water, before applying a few drops to the eyes! Agrimony was also used in poultices and compresses to heal wounds and snake bites and to stop bleeding due to its coagulant effect.

Agrimony has great anti-inflammatory properties and can be used to treat many gastrointestinal issues like mild diarrhea, and can reduce swelling of the gut and the soft tissues in the gastrointestinal tract. Agrimony can also be taken as tea in order to cleanse the liver and these cleansing properties can also help to soothe cystitis. When taking agrimony as a tea (see page 12) with a spoonful of honey, it can also ease a sore throat.

In the 18th-century Scottish Witch trial of Lilias Adie, agrimony was mentioned as a cure for anyone suffering from an unexplained illness, or elf shot, which was when a person or animal was believed to have been shot by an elf's arrow.

BASIL
Ocimum basilicum

FOLKLORE

There are 15 types of basil, the most common type being sweet basil. This green leafy herb has a rich and varied folklore and it carries diverse cultural and symbolic meanings in different parts of the world. The exact origins of basil aren't clear. Although the first historical record of basil was from the Hunan region of China in 807 AD, basil is thought to be native to India where it was used in sacred Hindu weddings and funerals, and in ceremonies to worship the god Vishnu. Holy basil is also a sacred Hindu herb that was believed to be a manifestation of the goddess Tulasi.

In Italian folklore, basil was seen as a symbol of love. Unmarried girls would wear a sprig of basil in their girdle while married women would wear basil behind their ears. Men would also wear basil on their hats as a symbol that they were ready to seek a wife. In Romanian folklore, basil was given by men as a proposal of marriage where the acceptance of a sprig of basil by a woman would mean the man would love her forever. In Greece, however, basil came to symbolize something very different—sorrow. It was also burned to cast out Witches. Basil didn't always represent love in other cultures either. In France, basil was sometimes known as "herb royale" as it was believed to have grown on the cross on which Christ was crucified. In other parts of Europe, basil was associated with the Devil and death. It was believed that the herb belonged to Satan and in order for it to grow and flourish, the ground had to be cursed before it was planted. In Egypt, basil was associated with death. The herb was found in tombs and was most likely used as part of the ritual to embalm and preserve the bodies of the dead.

ZODIAC SIGN
Scorpio
♏

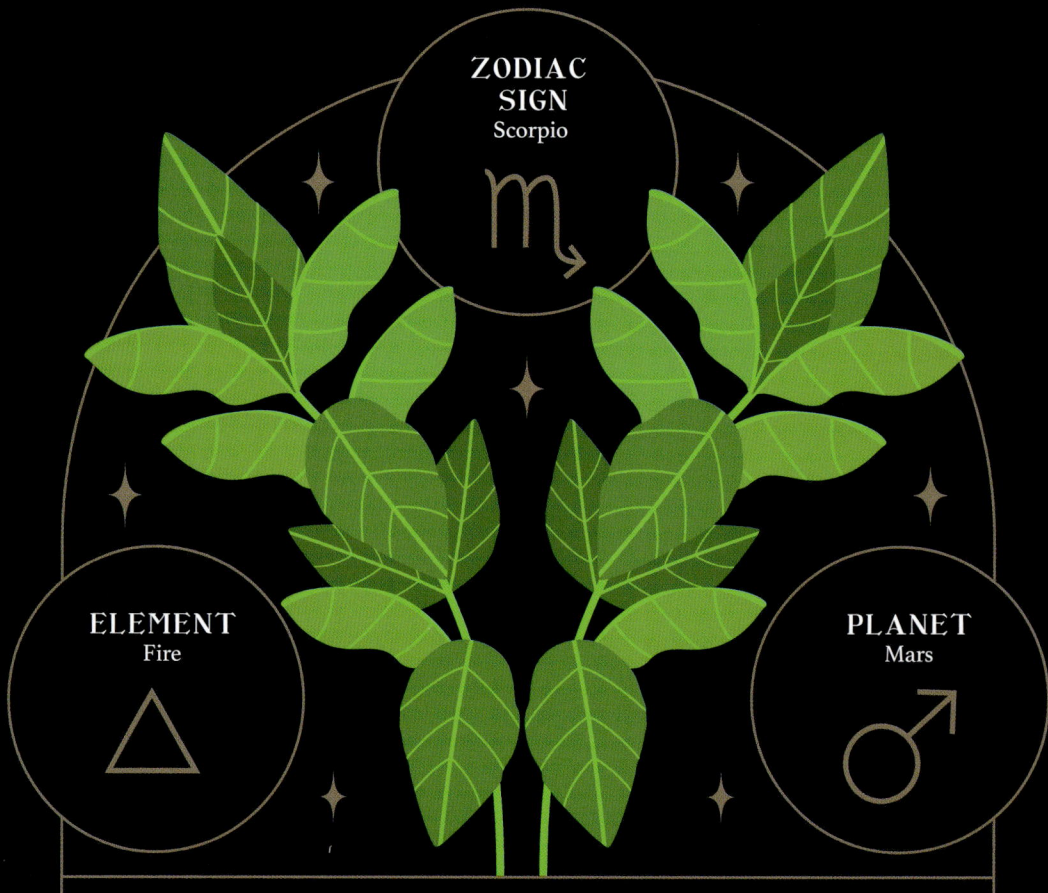

ELEMENT
Fire
△

PLANET
Mars
♂

BASIL
Ocimum basilicum

MAGICKAL PROPERTIES
- Boosts prosperity, abundance, and wealth
- Brings peace, courage, love, and protection
- Promotes astral travel and safe travel

MEDICINAL PROPERTIES
- Regulates blood sugar
- Soothes upset stomachs
- Heals infected cuts and stings
- Boosts immune system
- Cleanses the liver
- Reduces cholesterol
- Eases anxiety
- Soothes coughs
- Treats bronchitis

FOLK NAMES Alabahaca, American Dittany, Balanoi, Feslien, Herb of Kings, Njilika, Our Herb, St. Joseph's Wort, Sweet Basil, Tulsi, Witches Herb

MAGICKAL PROPERTIES

In magickal terms, basil is associated with prosperity, abundance, wealth, success, peace, courage, protection, and love. Place some dried basil in a pouch along with cinnamon, lavender, and rose to make a love charm that will bring you success in your romantic endeavors. Basil can also be used in love incenses, which seek to draw love toward you. Basil can bring financial success by keeping a leaf in your wallet to attract money. It can also be used to attract good luck and prosperity to a business by keeping a potted basil plant in areas where business is conducted, such as in a store, or by adding a sachet of dried basil to a cash register. Basil has strong protective qualities and was often scattered around homes to protect those who lived within it.

Basil is also associated with astral travel. According to folklore, if a Witch drinks basil oil or tea, it is a potent way in which to "hedge ride", which is a form of otherworldly travel where the hedge is a symbolic boundary between two worlds. To make basil oil, place 5 tsp of dried basil in 3 fl oz (100 ml) of sunflower, olive, or almond oil, and leave to infuse for 4 weeks. Drain the herbs from the oil before consuming. Add 1 tsp of this oil to basil tea (see page 12) to make it more potent. Since basil can aid astral travel in the metaphysical world, it can also aid safe travel in the physical realm. In England during the 1500s, a basil plant was given to guests to ensure a safe journey on their way home. Today, you can follow this tradition by keeping a sprig of basil somewhere about your person in a pouch when you travel, or by putting basil in your car to ensure you will safely reach your destination.

MEDICINAL PROPERTIES

Medicinally, basil has many uses. It's good for soothing an upset stomach, sore throats, nausea, and indigestion. It can also be used to help heal stings and infected cuts if used topically in a poultice (see page 28) as it possesses antibacterial and antimicrobial properties. Regularly eating basil in food brings a great deal of health benefits. It can help those who are looking to regulate their blood sugar levels by helping to manage a spike in glucose levels following a meal. Basil also contains antioxidants that can help to boost the immune system (particularly against viral infections) and reduce the impact of any ingested toxins that could cause liver damage. Consuming basil, either in food, tea, oil form, or as it is can assist with cholesterol management and can also help to regulate cortisol levels in the body to reduce feelings of anxiety. Holy basil can be taken as an tea to treat coughs and bronchitis. Place up to 10 fresh basil leaves in a cup of hot water and leave to steep for 5–7 minutes before drinking.

BAY LAUREL
Laurus nobilis

FOLKLORE

Bay laurel is an evergreen shrub and a popular kitchen herb native to the Mediterranean. Its leaves are shiny in appearance and are pointed, with the top side being darker than the underside. Sometimes called a bay tree or sweet bay, it produces greenish-yellow flowers in the springtime, producing berries after 3–4 years of cultivation.

Its folk history originates from the Romans and ancient Greeks. It's believed that the Greek god of the sun Apollo fell deeply in love with Daphne, a Greek Naiad nymph (a female spirit presiding over fountains, wells, and other bodies of water). But she did not love him in return. Her father, the river god Peneus, turned Daphne into a bay laurel tree to protect her from Apollo's unwanted advances. When Apollo found the bay laurel tree, he thought it was so beautiful that he used its branches to make the wreaths to honor the highest ancient Greek achievers, such as heroes, poets, returning soldiers, and newly qualified doctors as a symbol of their graduation success. This garland was known as *bacca laureus*, which over time became known as the baccalaureate, which we know today to be the name of a university degree. The ancient Greeks would also plant bay laurel trees at the side of their front door in order to protect them from Witches, sorcery, and demons.

In Roman folk history, it was believed that wherever a bay tree was planted, it would keep people safe from lightning strikes, which is why the emperor Tiberius would wear a crown of bay laurel leaves when it rained to prevent him from being struck by lightning. Roman gods also wore bay laurel wreaths as a symbol of honor, glory, and high status.

MAGICKAL PROPERTIES

Magickally, bay laurel leaves are associated with protection, success, courage, psychic abilities, wishes, money, and healing. When the leaves are burned as incense, the smoke created cleanses any harmful negative and unwanted energies from a room. The leaves can also be used to make wishes—simply write your wish on a bay laurel leaf and then burn it in a cauldron. In folklore,

ZODIAC SIGNS
Leo and Aries

ELEMENT
Fire

PLANET
The Sun

BAY LAUREL
Laurus nobilis

MAGICKAL PROPERTIES
- Brings protection and success
- Increases psychic abilities
- Boosts courage, money, healing, strength, and purification

MEDICINAL PROPERTIES
- Treats bronchitis
- Eases coughs
- Fights inflammation
- Eases bodily aches and pains
- Helps ease rheumatism
- Soothes insect bites and stings
- Eases colds and flu

FOLK NAMES Bair, Bay Laurel, Bay Tree, Daphne, Grecian Laurel, Laurel, Laurier d'Apollon, Laurier Sauce, Lorbeer, Nobel Laurel, Roman Laurel, Sweet Bay

the cauldron symbolizes the womb and is a tool of transformation through which our will is born. As you burn the leaf in your cauldron, visualize your wish coming true and as the leaf turns into smoke, your wish will be manifested.

Bay laurel leaves are also used to attract money. Simply place a leaf in your wallet to bring money into your life. To help attract more abundance and prosperity, you can also draw money sigils and signs on the leaf to aid your manifestations. Bay laurel is associated with psychic senses and can help with the development of your psychic abilities. Place 3 bay laurel leaves in a pouch along with 1 tsp each of mugwort, cinnamon, and marshmallow root, and then place the pouch under your pillow to aid psychic development as you sleep. To bring prophetic dreams, simply place 1 bay leaf in your pillowcase at night. Bay laurel can also help healers. When performing a healing spell or ritual, wear bay leaves as a necklace or simply carry some leaves in your pocket in order to amplify your magickal healing powers.

MEDICINAL PROPERTIES

Bay laurel has a long history in folklore for treating a variety of ailments. It can help when suffering from bronchitis, coughs, and flu. Take 4 drops of bay laurel oil either directly, in tea, or as an infusion (see page 12, 14, 18). The oil contains cineole, which has antibacterial and expectorant properties to aid healing of these kind of respiratory illness. In folk medicine, a syrup can be made into a paste from bay leaves and honey and applied to the chest to help with colds and coughs. The cineole in bay laurel may also help to fight inflammation by inhibiting the production of nitric oxide in the body, which at high concentrations can cause inflammation. Infusions, teas, and oils can also be taken to help in this way.

In folk medicine, bay leaves can also help to ease bodily aches. The best method to use to achieve this is to run a hot bath and place a handful of bay leaves in the water; as they soften and infuse the water, the oils that are released bring relief to pain in the limbs. Bay leaves can help with rheumatism too by making the leaves into a salve (see page 22) and rubbing onto the affected area. The softened leaves can also soothe insect bites and bee stings by placing them on the infected area as a poultice (see page 28).

CALENDULA
Calendula officinalis

FOLKLORE

Calendula, a part of the daisy family, is a herbaceous flowering plant with flat yellow and orange flowers used in ancient Greece, Egypt, and the Arabic empires. Sometimes known as marigold or Mary's gold, calendula, according to folklore, is one of the oldest plants known to folk medicine. It is generally cultivated as an ornamental and medicinal plant and is not usually found in any kind of wild or natural habitat. The flowers are edible and the ancient Greeks and Romans used them in cooking and as a garnish.

The folklore surrounding calendula comes from ancient Greece. There are many different legends surrounding this plant but all involve Apollo, the god of the sun. In one legend, Apollo was said to have fallen in love with a young maiden, but the strength of his affection, in the form of sun rays, was so strong that the maiden died. On the place of her death, it was said that calendula flowers began to bloom. Another legend tells of how four nymphs fell in love with Apollo, but unfortunately their jealousy was their undoing. They fought between them for Apollo's affection to the point where Apollo's sister, Artemis, turned them into calendula flowers to bring an end to the fighting.

MAGICKAL PROPERTIES

In magickal terms, calendula is associated with healing, happiness, protection, love, legal matters, prophetic dreams, and psychic abilities. It is also associated with solar magick, which is why the flowers are best picked once they are fully open in the afternoon on a sunny day when the sun is at the height of its power, as this helps to strengthen calendula's magickal (and medicinal) properties.

The flowers are believed to be highly protective against negative energy and intent, illness, and bad luck, and according to folklore, they can be made into garlands and hung from the front door handle of your home to protect those who live inside. Another old magickal charm using calendula flowers is to place them under your bed to protect against robbers and thieves while you sleep. If you are unfortunate enough to be robbed in the night, the flowers will illuminate the truth and help you identify the culprit in your dreams. Sleeping with calendula under your pillow helps to promote all forms of prophetic and lucky dreams.

The sunny, bright appearance of the calendula flower means it is magickally associated with happiness. They can be placed under the bed to ensure a happy and joyful marriage, which is why it was common in folklore to place the flowers in floral bridal headdresses. Calendula flowers were used in marriages in India, but they were also used in funeral ceremonies. Thanks to this, calendula can also be used in magickal rituals to remember loved ones that have passed. Calendula flowers are also thought to help you gain victory in any kind of legal matter. Carry the flowers in your pocket when in any legal situation, like in court, where you need a positive outcome.

MEDICINAL PROPERTIES

The ancient Egyptians would use calendula to treat skin complaints, and it is still used today to soothe skin irritations like sunburn, cuts, and scrapes, and to nourish dry skin and lips. The best way to do this is to use calendula oil. To make it, add dried calendula petals to olive, grapeseed, or avocado oil. Leave the petals to infuse in the oil for 4–6 weeks, shaking the bottle daily. After this time, strain out the herbs using a cheesecloth or sieve and pour the oil into another bottle. The oil is now ready to smooth onto all kinds of skin irritations. This oil is also suitable to ingest for gut health. Drink 3 drops in a cup of hot water to promote a healthy gut. This tea can also be taken as a tonic for lifting your mood.

The great herbalist Nicholas Culpeper wrote in the mid-1600s that distilled calendula flowers were used for "red and watery eies." To make a calendula mist to soothe sore eyes, bring a pan of water to the boil and then pour the water over a handful of calendula flowers and leave to steep for 15 minutes. After this time, remove the flowers and let the water cool completely. Pour the water into a spray bottle and use to spray on sore or red eyes to bring relief and reduce redness.

ZODIAC SIGN
Leo

ELEMENT
Fire

PLANET
The Sun

CALENDULA
Calendula officinalis

MAGICKAL PROPERTIES
- Promotes happiness, love, protection, and healing
- Guards against robbery
- Protects in legal matters
- Boosts prophetic dreams and psychic abilities

MEDICINAL PROPERTIES
- Treats dermatitis
- Soothes sunburn
- Nourishes dry skin
- Treats cuts and scrapes
- Lifts mood
- Reduces red and sore eyes
- Treats minor infections
- Reduces skin inflammation

FOLK NAMES Husbandman's Dial, Marybud, Marygold, Merrybud, Pot Marigold, Summer's Bride

ZODIAC SIGN
Leo

ELEMENT
Water

PLANET
The Sun

CHAMOMILE
Chamaemelum nobile and Matricaria recutita

MAGICKAL PROPERTIES
- Attracts prosperity, peace, blessings, beauty, and money
- Purifies and protects
- Aids dreamwork
- Honors the Sun

MEDICINAL PROPERTIES
- Calms and reduces anxiety
- Improves sleep
- Treats infection
- Treats flu
- Reduces menstrual pain
- Treats neuralgia
- Eases earache
- Reduces joint and muscle pain

FOLK NAMES
Ground Apple, Manzanilla, Maythen, Mayweed, Whig Plant

CHAMOMILE
Chamaemelum nobile & *Matricaria recutita*

FOLKLORE

There are two varieties of chamomile: Roman chamomile (*Chamaemelum nobile*) and German chamomile (*Matricaria recutita*). Both are native to southern and eastern Europe and western Asia, but have also been introduced into other temperate parts of the word. Chamomile can be commonly found in fields and meadows, on roadsides, and in other undisturbed areas. It has straggly stems with feathery leaves and a mass of daisy-like flowers with a fruity aroma. In ancient Greece, it was known as *chamomaela*, which translates as "ground apple".

The ancient Romans, Egyptians and Greeks all used this flower in their rituals and celebrations. The Egyptians used crushed chamomile flowers to illuminate the skin and to treat skin conditions. It was also used as an embalming oil and was burned to honour ancestors and the sun god Ra. The ancient Romans and Greeks used chamomile in tea to help reduce fevers and this herb has also been revered for centuries in Mexican and Native American folkloric traditions. Chamomile came into widespread use during the Middle Ages and many folk customs show the flowers and leaves of this plant were used for its protective qualities. It was also popular in Scandinavian countries where chamomile-infused water was used by the Vikings to rinse their hair to give it a beautiful shine.

MAGICKAL PROPERTIES

Chamomile has a wide variety of magickal properties including prosperity, protection, peace, blessings, dreamwork, attracting money, beauty, honouring the sun, and purification. In medieval folklore, chamomile was place near doors to protect against bad luck, as it acts as a guardian herb spirit when planted, which serves to protect your home against ill will and intent. You can also use a few drops of chamomile essential oil in water to wash your windows and doors to keep unwanted and negative energies from coming into your home. Another simple folk ritual for protection is to burn chamomile flowers inside your house to banish bad spirits.

To use chamomile, as the Egyptians did, to boost beauty, youth, and attractiveness, make a flower essence by placing fresh chamomile and lavender in a bowl or jar of water. Leave it to infuse in the sunlight for at least 3 hours when the sun is most energizing and powerful at midday. Drain the herbs and put the water into a spray bottle and use to mist the face in the morning and evening. Store in the refrigerator and use within 1 week.

In folk magick, chamomile was used to bring luck to gamblers. In order to get a magickal boost of luck, wash your hands in tea made from the flowers before taking part in any game of chance.

Chamomile has also been used for centuries to bring blessings, prosperity, and money. Dried chamomile can be hung in the home to attract these things toward you. You can also carry chamomile flowers with you in your pocket, or take a prosperity bath using chamomile, mint, basil, and bergamot (fresh, dried, or essential oils). Or, create an oil infusion (page 18) that can be used to anoint yourself or to use in spells and rituals for this purpose.

Chamomile is associated with dreamwork. It can be mixed with other herbs such as mugwort, cinquefoil, and yarrow and be taken as tea before bed or used in a dream pillow. You can also use these herbs in your bath. Place 3 tsp of each herb in a muslin bag and place in the hot water. Enjoy your bath for at least 20 minutes right before bedtime.

MEDICINAL PROPERTIES

Chamomile is a great remedy to reduce stress when taken as a tea. Make a tea (see page 12) with 2 tsp each of dried chamomile, lavender, and valerian to induce feelings of calm and to also improve sleep.

Chamomile is one of the "Nine Sacred Herbs" from the *Lacnunga*, an Old English herbal manuscript containing different kinds of Anglo-Saxon medical texts. These herbs are used in the old folk charm called the "Nine Herbs Charm," which was believed to treat any kind of infection and be a remedy for poison. You can find the instructions for this charm on page 106. To treat infection, mix the nine herbs (mugwort,

buckthorn, lamb's cress, nettle, betony, chamomile, crab apple, chervil, and fennel) with wood or charcoal ashes and water to form a paste and apply to the affected area. To counteract poison, mix with the nine herbs with apple juice to create a drink.

Chamomile can also be made into a salve (see page 22) and used for the treatment of pain such as earache or neuralgia. To ease bodily aches, sore muscles and joint, Chamomile can be made into a liniment (see page 25) that can be rubbed on any painful area to bring comfort and relief.

CILANTRO
Coriandrum sativum

FOLKLORE

A member of the parsley family, cilantro has a strong taste and smell. Known as one of the world's oldest herbs, it's native to the Mediterranean and the Middle East, but has spread to almost every other area of the globe. The ancient Romans were thought to have brought cilantro to as far west as Britain, where they used it with vinegar to preserve meat.

Cilantro is also known as coriander. The seeds of this plant have been found in ruins dating from 5000 BC in Egypt. In ancient Egyptian folklore, coriander seeds were used as an offering to the pharaohs in death due to their association with immortality. Some seeds were uncovered in the tomb of Tutankhamen when it was excavated.

In Chinese folklore, coriander seeds were also connected to immortality and were believed to have the power to grant life everlasting to anyone who ate them. There is even archaeological evidence of coriander seeds being found in a cave in Israel dating back to 6000 BC. The Israelites also used the seeds on the Passover table as mentioned in the Book of Exodus from the Bible which compared the seeds to manna, the spiritual food that God supplied to sustain his people.

During the medieval times and the Renaissance era, cilantro was used as an aphrodisiac and was added to love potions, as it was believed it heightened passion, particularly if drunk with wine.

MAGICKAL PROPERTIES

Cilantro has a wealth of magickal properties. In folklore, cilantro is most associated with love and passion. The powdered seeds can be added to wine and then drunk to induce lust. This wine can also be shared by two people who want to join together in love and align their souls to one another, which is a particularly powerful ritual to perform during the Full Moon. The seeds can also be added to love pouches along with pieces of ginger, red rose petals, and a cinnamon stick to enhance feelings of love and passion. Dried cilantro leaves can also be burned as incense along with red rose petals for the same purpose, and to induce feelings of lust.

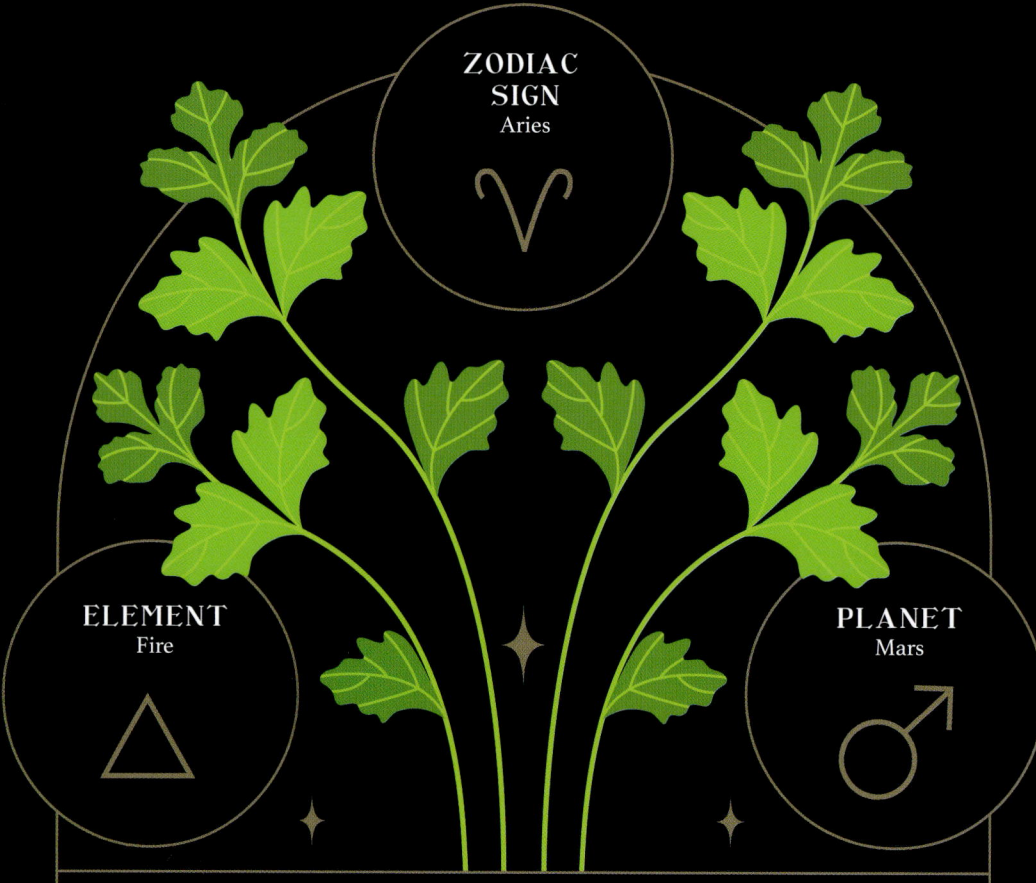

ZODIAC SIGN
Aries

ELEMENT
Fire

PLANET
Mars

CILANTRO
Coriandrum sativum

MAGICKAL PROPERTIES
- Brings love, lust, passion, protection, and reconciliation
- Promotes healing
- Stops fighting and arguments

MEDICINAL PROPERTIES
- Brings pain relief
- Aids digestion
- Relieves digestive discomfort
- Detoxifies

FOLK NAMES Chinese Parsley, Coriander, Dhania

Love and lust spells have been practiced since ancient times as one of the oldest forms of magick. Marcellus of Bordeaux, who used folk magick in the 4th century, suggested that to increase passion and love, the right testicle of a rooster (which was considered an aphrodisiac), should be worn in a pouch around the neck.

Cilantro can also be used in home protection spells and rituals and can be grown in your yard in order to protect your home and those who live within. Cilantro can also be gathered during harvest time and hung within the home for the same purpose.

Cilantro is also known for its powers of reconciliation and can bring people together who are having a difficult time getting along. The seeds can be crushed into a powder and added to any drink that is shared by those who are fighting in order to help overcome any issues. You can also put the seeds in a pouch along with a piece of rose quartz, lavender, and myrtle, and place it in the area where any talks of reconciliation may occur. Or, take it with you when you are likely to be in the same company of those you don't get along with to create a calm and peaceful environment.

MEDICINAL PROPERTIES

Cilantro is used for its antibacterial, antifungal, and antiseptic qualities. A poultice can be made from the leaves and can be placed on wounds to keep them free of infection (see page 28). A salve can also be made from a cup of cilantro leaves. Place them in a carrier oil such as sunflower or jojoba oil and leave them for 5 weeks, shaking the jar daily. Strain out the herbs and place the oil in a pan over a low heat. Add 1 oz (30 g) of beeswax, and stir everything well until it's mixed together completely. Place the mixture in a suitable container and once it's cooled and hardened, rub onto bites and cuts to keep them infection free.

Cilantro is known for its anti-inflammatory properties. To ease achy joints and muscles, place 1 tsp of ground-up seeds and 10 fl oz (300 ml) of oil and leave for 4 weeks. Strain the seeds. Once ready, rub onto joints to reduce inflammation and bring relief to painful muscles.

Known for its detoxifying qualities and its ability as a digestive aid, cilantro can be used in the form of a tea to help digestive issues and discomfort. Add 1 tsp of powdered seeds to a cup of hot water and leave to steep for 10 minutes before drinking. Drink this tea 2–4 times a day for detoxing and digestive purposes.

CLOVER
Trifolium repens

FOLKLORE

There are roughly 300 species of clover found around the world. The majority of clovers are trifoliate, meaning they have three leaves, but clovers with four, five, or more leaves can also be found. Many clovers have ball-like flowers in a range of different colors such as white, pink, red, and purple. They are native to Europe as well as central Asia, but have also been introduced to other countries around the world in the Northern Hemisphere. If you're foraging for clover, you're likely to find them in places such as yards, parks, waste grounds, and fields.

In folklore, three-leaf clovers are associated with a central belief in the Christian faith: the Holy Trinity, which represents the Father, the Son, and the Holy Spirit. In southern Ireland, where the majority of the population is Roman Catholic, the clover is the national symbol. It's believed that the patron saint Saint Patrick would use a three-leaf clover to explain the theology of the Holy Trinity, where God can manifest to humanity as God the Father, God the Son (Jesus), and God the Holy Spirit, in the same way that one clover has three leaves.

There are many legends associated with the humble clover and it can differ slightly depending on which area of the world the folklore originates. In Celtic folklore, a rhyme associates each leaf with a different aspect of life:

"One leaf for fame,
And one for wealth,
One for a faithful lover,
And one to bring you glorious health,
All in a four-leaf clover."

MAGICKAL PROPERTIES

In magickal terms, the three-leaf clover is associated with protection and can be worn as a protective amulet. In terms of number of leaves found on a clover, the three-leaf variety is the most common and can be used in any kind of protection spell or ritual—such as added to a protection pouch—and they can be crushed and used to dress a black candle for a quick and easy protection spell. Two-leaf clovers are far less common, but it is said that to find one means

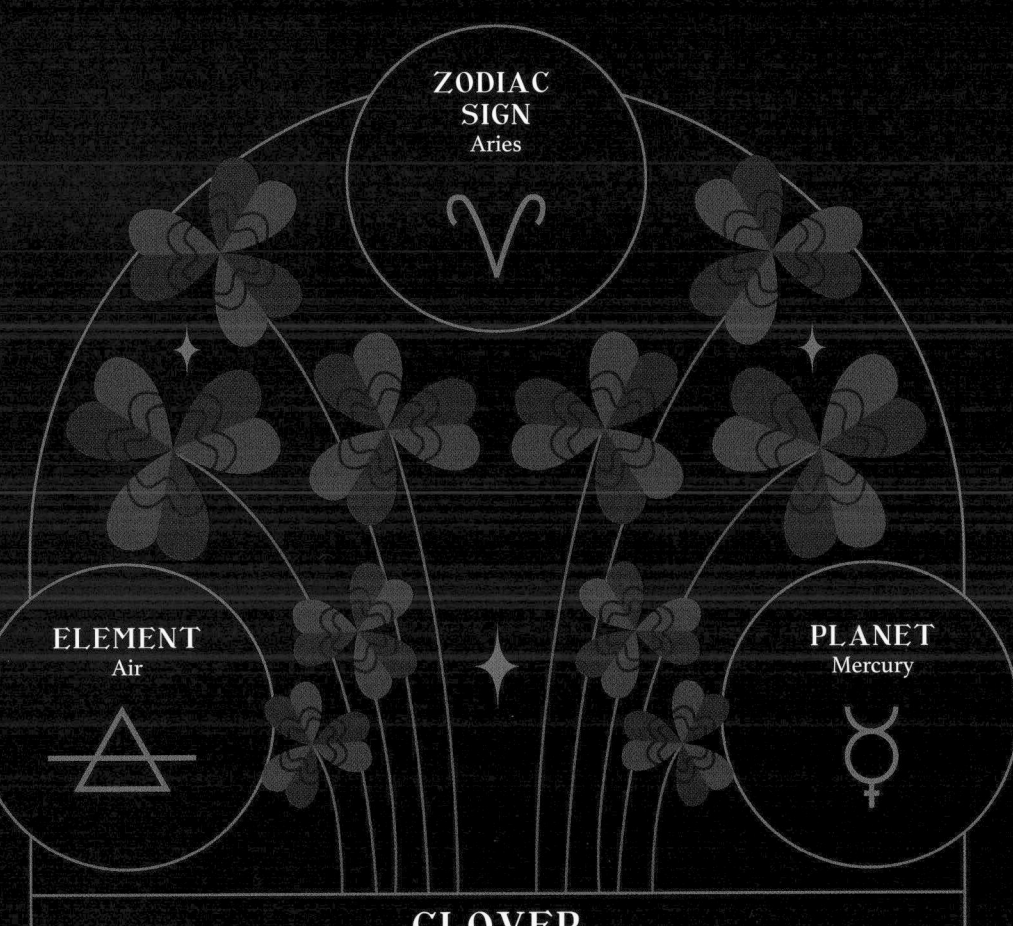

ZODIAC SIGN
Aries

ELEMENT
Air

PLANET
Mercury

CLOVER
Trifolium repens

MAGICKAL PROPERTIES
- Brings good luck, protection, love, money, and success

MEDICINAL PROPERTIES
- Exfoliates skin
- Treats eczema and acne
- Manages menopause symptoms
- Soothes sore throats
- Helps to combat colds
- Treats coughs and respiratory conditions

FOLK NAMES Honey, Honeystalks, Shamrock, Three-Leaved Grass, Trefoil, Trifoil

you will soon find a new lover. Five-leaf clovers, which are also much harder to find, symbolize attracting wealth and money, and the best way to take full advantage of its magickal attractive properties is to wear it in some way on the body.

The most prized of all clovers is the four-leaf variety, which is the bringer of good luck. According to folklore, it is associated with the cross on which Jesus Christ was crucified, and anyone who finds one will receive good fortune. It can also be used in spells and rituals to attract good luck. 17th century folklore tells us that the clover can be scattered on the path of a bride to bring her good luck in her marriage, and if an unmarried woman places a four-leaf clover in her shoe, she will soon marry.

A four-leaf clover can also be worn on your lapel to protect against being drafted into the military. To use it for this purpose, you can make a four-leaf clover oil and use it to anoint your pulse points, or make a four-leaf clover tea. Simply steep any number of clovers in hot (but not boiling) water for 5 minutes, or make a tea by leaving the clovers to steep in hot water for 15–20 minutes.

MEDICINAL PROPERTIES

Red clover has a wealth of medicinal properties. It contains salicylic acid, which can be used to exfoliate the skin to improve skin health and appearance. It can also be used in the treatment of acne and eczema. To make a treatment, place red clover and calendula in hot (but not boiling) water and leave to steep for 20 minutes. After this time, remove the plant matter, leave to cool, and then use the water to cleanse your face to sooth and treat skin complaints.

Red clover also contains isoflavones that act like the estrogen hormone, which can help manage symptoms of menopause such as hot flushes, depression, and anxiety. One of the best ways to take red clover for this purpose is by drinking it in tea daily. Take a few red clover flowers and let them steep in hot (but not boiling) water for at least 5 minutes before drinking.

Red clover is traditionally used to help colds, sore throats, coughs, bronchitis, and other respiratory conditions due to its antimicrobial properties. It can be made into a tincture (see page 20) which is taken internally. After making your red clover tincture, you can take 10–20 drops, three times a day, either directly under your tongue, or in your drinks.

DISCLAIMER:
Check with your doctor before consuming red clover if you are taking birth control, or have or have previously had breast cancer.

COMFREY
Symphytum officinale

FOLKLORE

Comfrey has been grown for over 2,000 years for its many culinary, medical, and magickal uses. Its flowers are small and bell-shaped, which are usually white or pink in color, and the plant itself grows up to 3 ft (1 m) in height. Comfrey grows in countries such as Europe, North America, Australia, and western Asia.

The ancient Greeks used comfrey from around 400 BC, and the Greek physicians Herodotus and Pedanius Dioscorides grew comfrey to use as medicines to heal. Comfrey's name stems from the Latin word *Symphytum*, meaning "to grow together," or the Greek word *sympho*, meaning "to unite," so it's easy to see why the ancient Greeks believed it had the power to heal fractures. Comfrey was used in many other cultures including Slavic countries, in traditional Chinese medicine, and in Native American traditions as it was valued for its healing abilities. In Celtic traditions, comfrey was also considered a sacred herb to the goddess Brigid and was used frequently in healing rituals.

In medieval England, monks would use comfrey as a way to stop bleeding and to treat hernias. Comfrey appears in many monastic texts because monks grew their own comfrey within the grounds of their monasteries to treat, in particular, the wounds of soldiers coming back from battle.

MAGICKAL PROPERTIES

Comfrey can be used for protection, specifically from theft. A little piece can be placed in your home near the front door, or you can make a pouch with comfrey, rose thorns, and iron nails to protect yourself or your home from thieves. Comfrey also helps to protect travellers. Carry dried comfrey in your pocket as you travel to ensure your safety, or place some in your suitcase to protect it from getting stolen or lost.

Comfrey can also be used in spells to manifest long-term goals. Anoint a candle with a little oil and roll it in ground-up comfrey leaves, burning it to help focus your intentions on manifesting your goals.

Comfrey can also be used to bring abundance and luck to gamblers. Wrap the money you intend to gamble with in comfrey leaves to help bring you good fortune, luck, and

ZODIAC SIGN
Capricorn

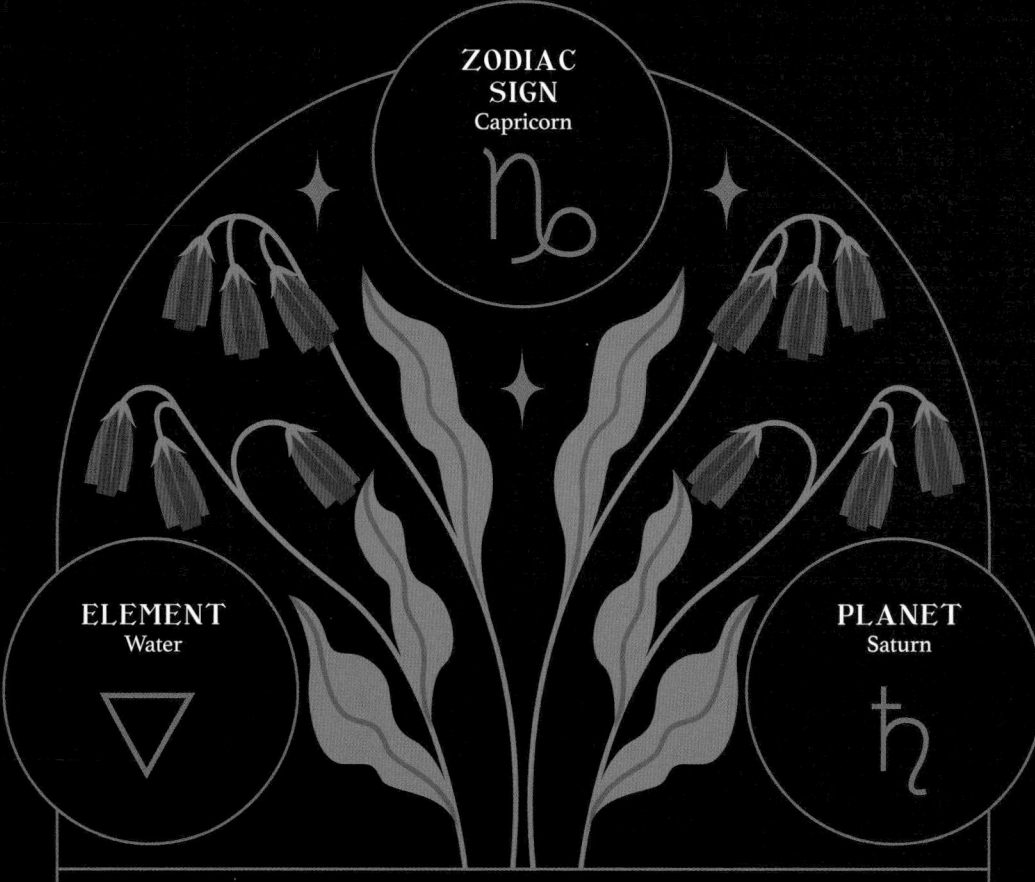

ELEMENT
Water

PLANET
Saturn

COMFREY
Symphytum officinale

MAGICKAL PROPERTIES
- Protects against thieves
- Manifests long term goals
- Brings luck, good fortune, success, and money
- Promotes safe travel and concentration when driving

MEDICINAL PROPERTIES
- Stops bleeding
- Treats bruises
- Heals abscesses
- Heals bone fractures and breaks

FOLK NAMES Boneset, Black Wort, Bruisewort, Consound, Gavez, Karakaffes, Knitbone, Slippery-Root

success. It can also help with concentration when practicing divination. Divination is the practice of discovering hidden knowledge or foretelling the future using tools such as tarot and oracle cards or runes. A simple folk use of comfrey for this purpose is to combine it with mugwort. You can place these herbs together in a pouch and carry it with you while you divine, and you can also use these herbs to dress a purple candle (anointing with a little oil before you roll the candle in the herbs) and let it burn during your divination practice. A tea can also be made from comfrey and mugwort that can be drunk before and during divination. Just make sure this tea isn't consumed more than once a month, and not on a regular basis (see below).

MEDICINAL PROPERTIES

Comfrey can be used in poultices to stop heavy bleeding and treat bruises and abscesses. The leaves can be boiled down to a glue-like substance that can be applied to any wound to bind it together and stop it bleeding. Comfrey can also be taken as a tisane or tincture to help wounds heal faster (see pages 17 and 20). Comfrey also possesses anti-inflammatory properties so is good to use as a poultice on inflamed joints or wounds, or to treat rheumatism and help with pain (see page 28). To create a comfrey salve to rub on wounds, place 2 cups of comfrey leaves in a carrier oil such as sunflower or jojoba oil in an airtight jar and leave for 5 weeks, shaking the jar daily. Drain the leaves and place the oil in a double boiler or in a heat-proof bowl placed over a pan of water on a low heat. Add 1 oz (30 g) of beeswax, making sure the wax melts down completely into the oil. Then place in a container (you could reuse an old lip balm tin). Use once it's cooled and hardened, and use within 1 year.

Comfrey can be used to help heal bone fractures too, allowing the bone to grow back stronger. In the 16th century, the herbalist Nicholas Culpeper said of comfrey, "It is said to be so powerful to consolidate and knit together." To use it for this purpose, Culpeper noted that comfrey could be taken as a syrup (see page 27) to heal "inwards hurts" like broken bones and internal injuries.

DISCLAIMER:
It is important to note that if comfrey is consumed weekly over a period of six months, it can be toxic to the liver due the alkaloids present in the leaves. However, it is perfectly safe to use comfrey tea, tincture, syrups, and decoctions very sparingly (only once a month) safely and with no side effects.

FENNEL
Foeniculum vulgare

FOLKLORE

A member of the carrot family, fennel has long stalks that grow up to 7 ft (2 m) in height and forms a bulb that grows above ground. At the tip of the stalk there are light, feathery leaves, and when fennel goes to seed, it produces yellow flowers. Native to southern Europe, it is now naturalized in northern Europe, north America, and Australia and is cultivated around the globe.

In folklore, fennel was often called "the snake herb," as it was believed that snakes would get better eyesight simply by rubbing up against it. This might explain why in 1 AD the ancient Roman naturalist Pliny recommended fennel for eyesight in his book *Natural History*. Due to its name as "the snake herb," Fennel was also believed to be a remedy for snakebites.

In ancient Greek mythology, Prometheus, the son of the Titan Lapetus, was believed to have taken a spark from the fire of the gods in a hollow stalk of fennel, as he wanted to give the gift of fire to mankind against Zeus's wishes. When Zeus found out, he punished Prometheus by creating the woman Pandora, giving her a box that he told her never to open. Unfortunately, she opened it, and out came the world's evils, woes, hardships, and diseases to plague humanity. As a plant sacred to the fire gods, fennel was also used to channel the divine and for gaining divine insight.

Fennel is one of the herbs in The Nine Herbs Charm, a 10th-century Anglo-Saxon charm, which was made as an antidote to poison and was thought to heal all infections (see page 106).

MAGICKAL PROPERTIES

Fennel is highly protective and can be hung in your house at doorways and windows to protect your home from evil, unwanted visitors, and malicious magick. A traditional Midsummer herb, it is particularly potent if you hang the plant in your home on Midsummer's Eve. Dried fennel seeds can also be burned as incense in your home to clear any lingering negative energy and purify the air, adding further home protection.

ZODIAC SIGN
Virgo
♍

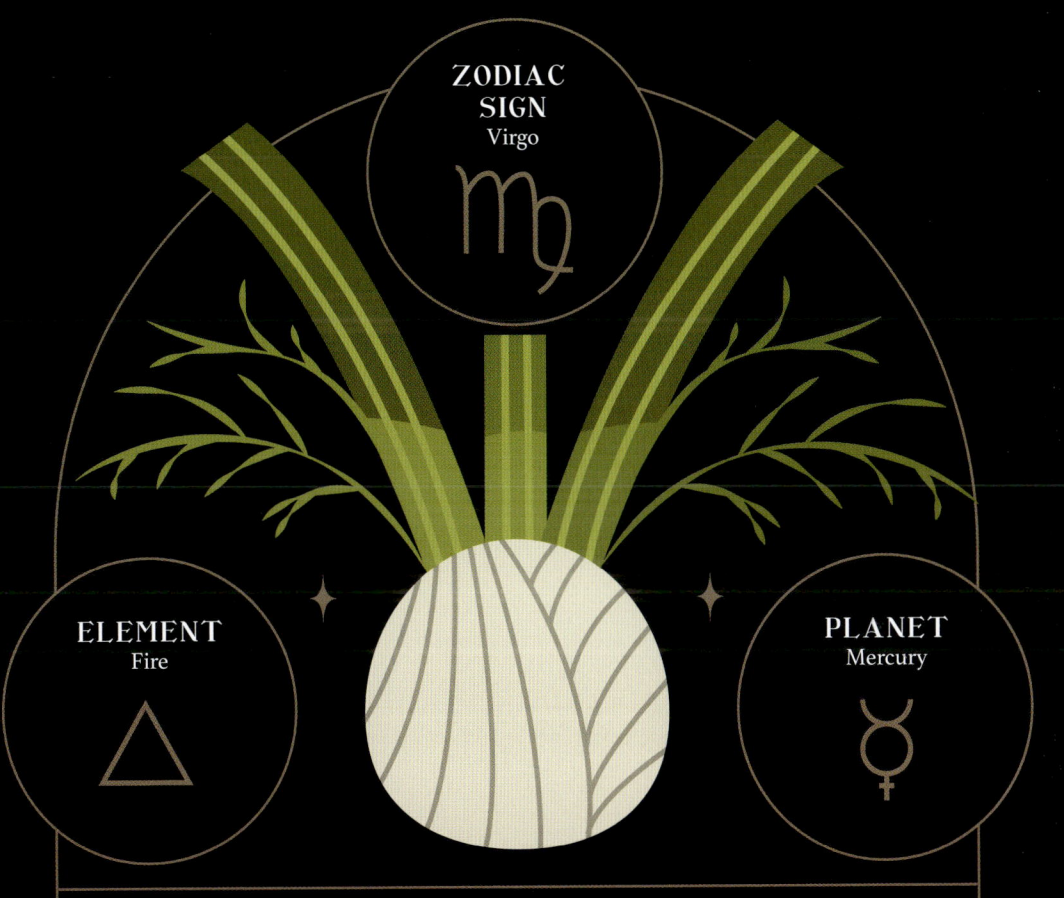

ELEMENT
Fire
△

PLANET
Mercury
☿

FENNEL
Foeniculum vulgare

MAGICKAL PROPERTIES
- Protects
- Clears negative energy
- Purifies
- Enhances psychic abilities, memory, courage, strength, and confidence
- Boosts fertility and longevity

MEDICINAL PROPERTIES
- Detoxifies
- Reduces water retention
- Suppresses appetite
- Relieves menopause symptoms
- Helps manage painful periods
- Acts as a milk stimulant for lactating parents

FOLK NAMES Bitter Fennel, Fenkel, Samar, Sheer, Sweet Fennel, Wild Fennel

Fennel can also be used to enhance psychic abilities by burning a mixture of fennel seeds and mugwort during meditation practices, and when practising any form of divination and during any spell or ritual aligned with this purpose. When fennel is combined and burned together with lemon peel, lavender, rosemary, and dill seeds, it can help to enhance your memory as well as offer an uplifting boost.

Fennel is known to bring courage and strength. To summon the courage you need, roll a red candle in a carrier oil such as sunflower or jojoba oil and then dress it with ground-up fennel seeds. As the candle burns, visualize drawing strength and courage toward you. After the candle has burned out, bury the remnants somewhere on your property to continue to bring this kind of energy into your life. You can also chew a few fennel seeds before you do anything that requires courage, and if you need a boost of confidence, carry some fennel seeds in your pocket.

Fennel is magickally associated with fertility and longevity when consumed, and the seeds can also can be used as an aphrodisiac when included in love spells and rituals.

MEDICINAL PROPERTIES

Fennel is good for digestion. To make a digestion tea, add 1 tsp each of crushed fennel seeds, cumin, and cumin seeds in a cup of hot water and leave to brew for 5–10 minutes before drinking to improve digestion, as well as detoxify the body. Take 2–3 times a day. Fennel seeds drunk as tea on their own can also help with water retention, can help to supress your appetite if you're looking to lose weight, and may help to relieve the symptoms associated with the menopause and perimenopause, such as hot flushes. It can also help with the management of painful periods and polycystic ovary syndrome.

Fennel can be used to treat respiratory diseases such as bronchitis when made into a tincture (see page 20) and taken in a drink, in food, or placed under the tongue 3–4 times a day. It is also highly nutritious and is packed with vitamin C, magnesium, potassium, antioxidants, and fibre, which can benefit heart health and help to reduce risk factors like high cholesterol.

Tea has long been a popular way to take herbs for their medicinal properties, but for some Witches, it has not always ended well. In the early 17th century, Joan, Margaret, and Philippa Flower from Belvoir in Leicestershire, who were known for their healing powers, gave herbal tea to heal the children of the Earl and Countess of Rutland. The healers were accused of Witchcraft when two of the sons died as a result of their illness.

FEVERFEW
Tanacetum parthenium

FOLKLORE

Part of the daisy family, feverfew is commonly found along roadsides and in yards. It has yellow-green leaves and is strongly aromatic, especially when the leaves are crushed. Native to the Balkan Peninsula, feverfew can now be found in the rest of Europe, North America, and Australia.

In medieval Europe, feverfew was planted near the front door of a house to protect the inhabitants from the plague, making it a popular plant to grow in cottage gardens. It was also considered a protective herb against the unwanted interference of the Fae, particularly on Midsummer's Eve. As well as protection, feverfew was considered a potent herb by horsemen. In East Anglia in England, during the 16th century, feverfew was used to soothe the temperaments of unruly horses who could not be calmed or tamed. The ancient Greeks also used feverfew, along with hyssop and rosemary, to save the lives of workers who fell from the Parthenon during its construction in the 5th century BC.

In Anglo-Saxon England, feverfew was believed to be a cure for the aliment elf-shot. This was caused by elves who shot flint tipped arrows into people and animals, particularly cattle. This would cause pain in localized areas where the arrows hit. In the Anglo-Saxon book the *Lacnunga*, feverfew, red nettles, and plantain were boiled together in butter and applied to the affected area to help cure the pain. It was believed that because these herbs have spear-headed leaves, they would counteract the impact of elf-shot.

MAGICKAL PROPERTIES

Feverfew is known for its protective qualities and is a powerful shield against any kind of negative energy or ill intent. Feverfew leaves can be carried in a pouch as an amulet for any kind of personal protection, or can be hung next to the door of your house for home protection. For extra home protection and to prevent illness of the inhabitants within, feverfew can be grown in your yard.

This herb can also be used in banishing spells. Grind down feverfew leaves along with rosemary and common garden sage in a mortar and pestle and then use them with some oil to dress a black candle. Dress a candle by covering your candle with oil and then roll it in the herbs so that they stick to it. Once the candle has fully burned out, bury the remnants somewhere away from your home and property to banish unwanted or negative energies that may have become attached to you.

As the ancient Greeks used feverfew as a protective charm during the construction of the Parthenon to save the lives of fallen workers, feverfew, along with hyssop and rosemary, can be used magickally today in a charm bag to protect against general accidents. To protect against any accidents while traveling, feverfew can be placed in a pouch with a St Christoper medal (the patron saint of travelers) and comfrey root and carried with you, stored somewhere in your car, or placed in your suitcase.

MEDICINAL PROPERTIES

Feverfew has been used in folk medicines for more than 2,000 years. The Greek physician Pedanius Dioscorides used feverfew in 60 AD for "all inflammations," and it can be used to treat inflammatory conditions such as rheumatoid arthritis. To treat inflammation, a cold compress can be made by soaking a cloth in feverfew tisane or oil and applied directly on the inflamed area to lessen the swelling. As its name suggests, feverfew was used to cure fevers. A hot compress can be made by heating the tisane in a pan until it's warm, then soaking a cloth in the liquid. It can then be applied to the forehead to draw out the heat in the body associated with a fever.

Feverfew can help with the pain of menstrual cramps to due its anti-inflammatory properties, which reduces inflammation in the uterine lining that causes pain. For this purpose, eat 2–3 feverfew leaves a day for 3–4 days before your period or when you usually start to suffer from menstrual cramps.

Feverfew is an effective migraine medicine. It's possible that the accumulative effects of this plant reduce the muscle spasms that are part of many forms of migraine. To treat migraines, eat 3 small fresh or dried feverfew leaves, each about 1.5 in (4 cm) long, each day. The leaves can be eaten on their own or put in food if you want to mask the bitter taste. It's possible that following this routine for 2 months will have a significant impact on those suffering with migraines.

DISCLAIMER:
Feverfew can be used to bring on a delayed period, but must be avoided during pregnancy.

ZODIAC SIGN
Taurus and Libra

ELEMENT
Water

PLANET
Venus

FEVERFEW
Tanacetum parthenium

MAGICKAL PROPERTIES
- Protects
- Prevents illness
- Can be used in banishing spells
- Purifies
- Prevents accidents
- Promotes safe travel

MEDICINAL PROPERTIES
- Treats swelling
- Cures fevers
- Relieves pain from menstrual cramps
- Treats migraines and headaches

FOLK NAMES Devil Daisy, Featherfew, Featherfoil, Featherfully, Febrifuge Plant, Flirtwort, Maid's Weed, Matricaria, Missouri Snakeroot, Nosebleed, Prairie-Dock, Rainfarn, Vetter-Voo, Wild Chamomile

JUNIPER
Juniperus communis

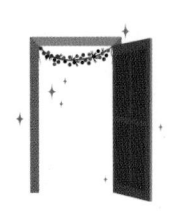

FOLKLORE

Juniper is a member of the cypress family and is an evergreen conifer that can be found throughout the Northern Hemisphere. It has needle-like leaves and the female plant of the common juniper produces bluish-black berries that have been used in folkloric medicine for thousands of years. Not all juniper berries are edible, but the ones from the common juniper plant are most frequently used in food, drink, and medicinal preparations.

In ancient Egypt, the oil from the juniper berry was used to anoint bodies and in the mummification process in order to preserve the bodies of the dead, and to ensure their spiritual body would continue to exist in the afterlife. When Tutankhamen's tomb was excavated in the 1920s, juniper berries were found in his sarcophagus, as it was also believed that the berries would enable the souls of the dead to mature until they could be reincarnated.

The ancient Greeks believed juniper berries could aid with physical endurance and stamina, and because of this, were often consumed during the Olympics and other sporting events and activities.

In European folklore, juniper was believed to have great purification properties and was ritually thrown into Beltane fires in order to purify people and their homes. It was also believed that this would help to purify animals and protect them from getting sick. Burning juniper wasn't just thought to protect animals from illness, but when people breathed in the smoke, it was thought it would protect them from catching the plague. It was also believed that juniper would protect against any kind of evil spirits or malevolent magick, and that when hung in the doorway of the home, it would force Witches to count every leaf before entering.

MAGICKAL PROPERTIES

From folklore, it's clear that juniper is an excellent purifier. The needles can be burned as incense within the home to purify the air and cleanse it from any negative energy, and it is a good herb to burn to purify and cleanse sacred spaces and tools or items used in spell and ritual

ZODIAC SIGNS
Leo and Aries

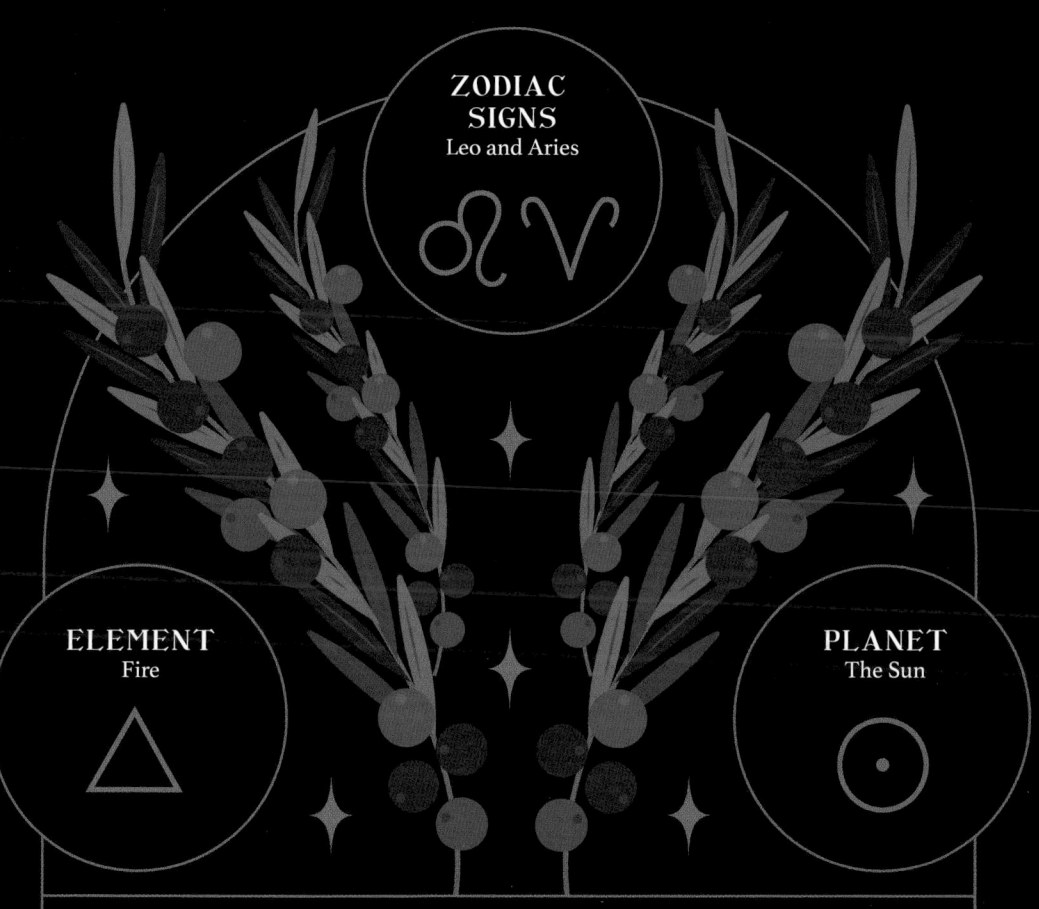

ELEMENT
Fire

PLANET
The Sun

JUNIPER
Juniperus communis

MAGICKAL PROPERTIES
- Purifies
- Cleanses magickal tools
- Protects
- Attracts good health and good luck

MEDICINAL PROPERTIES
- Boosts immune system
- Promotes good heart health
- Reduces inflamed muscles and joints
- Promotes calm
- Reduces anxiety
- Induces relaxation

FOLK NAMES Enebro, Gin Berry, Gin Plant, Geneva, Gemeiner, Wachholder

work. Burning this herb also helps to increase psychic abilities. A juniper infusion can also be made and used to wash magickal tools, altars, ritual spaces, floors in your home, and your front door and windows to prevent malevolent spirits entering your house. A sprig can be hung about the entrance to your home to protect it from ill intent and negative energy.

Juniper is highly protective. This plant can be of great use for travel protection and can be added to a pouch and placed in your car to prevent accidents. An old folkloric charm for travel protection also includes tying seven knots in a piece of red string and then using this to tie up seven juniper twigs to hang on your rearview mirror.

Juniper might cleanse unwanted and negative energies, but is also well known for its ability to attract good health and luck. Plant a juniper plant in your yard to bring good luck into your home or put some needles and berries in a pouch, and take it with you if you need an extra boost of good luck.

MEDICINAL PROPERTIES

Juniper berries have many medicinal uses. They are full of antioxidants and vitamin C, which can be used to boost your immune system and promote good health when taken as a syrup, particularly in the winter months when coughs and colds are more prevalent. To make a syrup, boil the berries in water on a low heat for 20-25 minutes, strain out the berry mush and seeds leaving just the water, then add equal amounts of water and honey into the liquid left behind. Put back on a low heat until it becomes thick in consistency. Take 1 tbsp of the syrup once a day. The high level of antioxidants can also help keep the heart healthy too.

As an oil, the antioxidants in the juniper berry can help reduce inflammation. The berries can be placed in an airtight jar with a carrier oil such as sunflower or jojoba oil and left to infuse for 4 weeks, shaking daily, before using the oil to rub on painful and inflamed areas of the body like joints and muscles. Taking the berries in food and as a tea can also help to tackle inflammation.

Using juniper essential oil in aromatherapy can help to bring calm, reduce anxiety, and induce relaxation when inhaled (essential oils should not be ingested or applied directly to the skin).

DISCLAIMER:
Avoid juniper during pregrancy.

LAVENDER
Lavandula angustifolia

FOLKLORE

Part of the mint family, lavender is an evergreen shrub with grey-green long leaves and purple flowers. Native to the Mediterranean and the Middle East, it has since spread throughout the world and now there are about 30 species of lavender, with the most common being English and French varieties.

Lavender is one of the world's best-known herbs and has been used for over 2,000 years. Its oil was used in ancient Egypt during the mummification process and it was used in bathhouses in ancient Rome because of its beautiful scent. Lavender is also mentioned in the Bible. Referred to as spikenard (or just nard), it was used in the expensive ointment used by Mary to anoint the feet of Jesus. The Romans changed the name to lavender, which comes from the Latin word *lavare*, meaning "to wash."

In medieval and Renaissance Europe, lavender had a close association with washing as well as bathing. Washerwomen were commonly known as lavenders during this time because they would wash clothes and lay them on lavender bushes so that as they dried, they would absorb the fragrance. In 17th-century France, Louis XIV was also known to use lavender oil to scent his bathwater.

During the 14th century, lavender was used in Portugal and Spain to ward off evil and would be included as part of bonfires during St John's Day (June 24), and on St Luke's Day (October 18). In Europe, lavender was also used by maidens who would put it under their pillows in the hopes that it would help them to dream about their true love. Lovers would also exchange lavender as a symbol of love and devotion.

MAGICKAL PROPERTIES

Lavender is used in all kinds of spells and rituals associated with bringing calm, happiness, and peace. For this purpose, make a ritual bath blend including equal parts of lavender, chamomile, passionflower, and lemon balm by putting these herbs into a muslin or organza pouch, and placing it in your bath water. You can also use dried lavender or essential oil to dress a white candle and burn it for calmness and peace. This can also help you to focus during meditation.

Lavender is known for its ability to ward off nightmares and can be added to a pillow with 1 tbsp of juniper leaves, 3 bay leaves, and 1 tbsp of thyme to stop unpleasant dreams when placed under your pillow at night. Lavender can be used alone in a dream pillow to help to unlock your unconscious mind and raise awareness as you sleep, and promote lucid dreams.

Lavender enhances psychic abilities. It can be burned as incense when performing spells and rituals associated with raising psychic awareness. Dried lavender or lavender essential oil can be used to anoint a purple candle and burned to help give a boost of power to your psychic abilities. Lavender essential oil diluted in a carrier oil can also be rubbed between the brows to help open the Third Eye.

Lavender may not be the first herb that comes to mind when thinking about protection, but it can help to ward off harmful influences and negative energy due to its subtle protective properties. Fresh or dried lavender can be carried or worn as an amulet, or 5 drops of lavender essential oil can be added to 0.6 fl oz (20 ml) of carrier oil and used to anoint your pulse points for personal protection.

MEDICINAL PROPERTIES

Lavender is well known for its ability to alleviate anxiety, as simply smelling its scent can relieve feelings of stress. It can even help depression and provide a great mood boost. Carry a bottle of lavender essential oil in your pocket to smell when needed, burn lavender essential oil in an oil burner, or use it in incense in the home to help combat anxiety and promote a stress-free environment. Smelling lavender in these ways can also help to soothe headaches and treat exhaustion.

Lavender can help treat insomnia. Drinking a combination of lavender, hops, passionflower, and chamomile tea before bed can encourage a good night's sleep, and a salve can be made from the same herbs that can be rubbed on the temples before sleep (see page 22).

Due to its antibacterial and antiseptic properties, lavender can be used to treat wounds, insect bites, and burns. A common external treatment to combat infection is to apply a few drops of diluted lavender oil directly onto the affected area (see page 18). To fight infection internally, lavender, cinnamon bark, rosemary, red sandalwood, and nutmeg can be left to macerate together in red wine for a week to produce a tincture known as red lavender. Take 30–60 drops, split over 3–6 doses a day, either directly under the tongue or in a drink.

Lavender also has anti-inflammatory and pain-relieving qualities. A lavender massage oil can be rubbed onto inflamed joints, and can reduce the pain associated with sore and aching muscles.

ZODIAC SIGNS
Gemini and Virgo

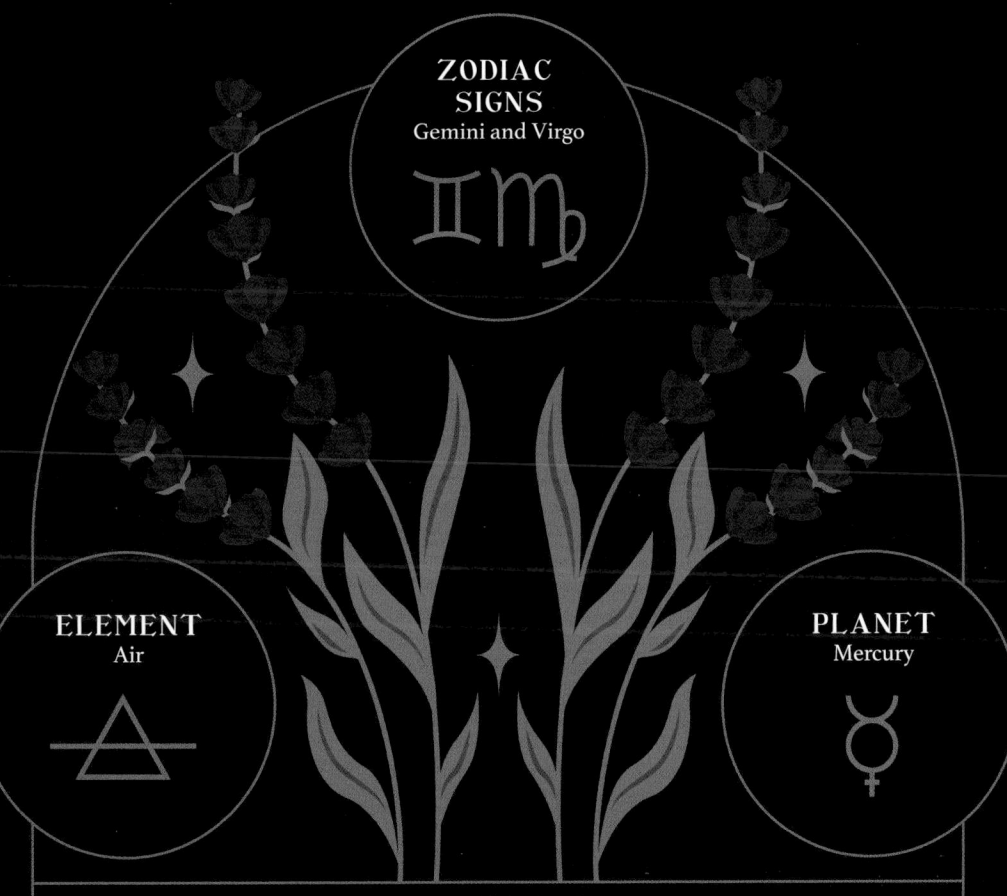

ELEMENT
Air

PLANET
Mercury

LAVENDER
Lavandula angustifolia

MAGICKAL PROPERTIES
- Promotes calm, peace, and happiness
- Wards off nightmares
- Promotes lucid dreaming
- Enhances psychic abilities
- Opens the Third Eye
- Protects
- Wards off harmful energies

MEDICINAL PROPERTIES
- Alleviates anxiety
- Reduces stress
- Helps depression
- Boosts mood
- Eases insomnia
- Relieves sore or aching muscles

FOLK NAMES Elfleaf Nard, Nardus, Spike

ZODIAC SIGN
Cancer

ELEMENT
Water

PLANET
Jupiter

LEMON BALM
Melissa officinalis

MAGICKAL PROPERTIES
- Attracts love
- Brings happiness
- Attracts prosperity
- Purifies
- Brings success
- Boosts confidence
- Helps dream manifestation

MEDICINAL PROPERTIES
- Reduces anxiety and stress
- Improves sleep
- Improves digestion
- Aids relaxation
- Enhances concentration
- Lifts the mood
- Reduces muscles and joint pain

FOLK NAMES Balm, Bee Balm, Heart's Delight, Honey Balm, Lemon Balsam, Melissa, Oghoul, Sweet Balm, Sweet Melissa, The Elixir of Life, Tourengane

LEMON BALM
Melissa officinalis

FOLKLORE

Lemon balm is a bushy herb native to Europe, north Africa and west Asia, although it now grows all over the world. Part of the mint family, lemon balm has broad heart-shaped, serrated-edged leaves that release a lemon fragrance when crushed or rubbed. In the spring and summer, it has clusters of small light yellow and white flowers that grow from where the leaves meet the stem.

The ancient Greeks knew lemon balm as *Melissa*, which means "honey bee," because the small flowers attracted bees and were commonly planted around beehives. In Greek mythology, Melissa was also the name of the nymph who discovered honey and was able to take the form of a bee. Melissa also used honey to nurse the infant Zeus so that he was later able to gain his power to become king of the gods. Bees were also sacred to the Greek goddess Artemis and many priestesses who served her were given "bee" as a title to honor them. The Oracle at Delphi was also called "bee" and it was from this that lemon balm became associated with immortality, power, and the unknown.

One of the first recorded uses of lemon balm came from the ancient Greek physician Pedanius Dioscorides who used it in wine to bring about calm. In the 1600s, herbalist Nicholas Culpeper wrote in his book *Complete Herbal* that lemon balm was associated with the zodiac sign Cancer and the element Water, and when mixed with honey, had the ability to affect and calm emotions.

MAGICKAL PROPERTIES

Lemon balm is associated with love and happiness and can be used to attract love into your life. Brew 1 tsp of lemon balm in 8.5 fl oz (250 ml) white wine for a few hours and drink it with someone to bring more love into the relationship. Sharing this wine with friends can also help to cement the bonds of friendship. Lemon balm is used in love spells and can be placed in a pouch with hawthorn leaves, rose petals, and rosemary to help heal a broken heart.

Lemon balm can also bring happiness into your life. Hang some lemon balm in your house to help create a happy home environment. In addition to this, lemon balm can attract by burning a green candle dressed with crushed lemon balm in your home, and burying the remnants somewhere on your property in order to bring prosperity to all who live there.

Lemon balm can be used for purification. It can be burned as incense to purify a space and can be added to water and used as a floor wash to cleanse your home. Lemon balm can also be added to ritual baths for purification purposes along with cilantro, peppermint, and parsley.

This herb is known for its ability to bring success and confidence. Carry some lemon balm leaves with you whenever you need a boost of confidence. The leaves can also be carried in your pocket when sitting an exam or going for a job interview to make sure your endeavors are successful.

Lemon balm is associated with dream manifestation. To manifest your dreams, write them down on a piece of paper, placing it in a pouch with dried lemon balm leaves and carry it with you until your dreams become a reality.

MEDICINAL PROPERTIES

Lemon balm is a calming herb that can help to reduce anxiety, stress, and improve sleep. To make a tincture to ease anxiety, place a cup full of chopped lemon balm leaves in an airtight jar with 40% proof alcohol (like vodka or brandy) so the leaves are fully submerged. Leave the jar for a month to infuse, shaking it daily. Strain away the leaves before using your tincture, taking 15 drops 3 times a day.

Making tinctures was a common practice among healers and Witches. In 1576, an Ayrshire woman called Bessie Dunlop was accused of Witchcraft, and at her trial she spoke of how she used traditional folk medicines, making tinctures as well as poultices and ointments to heal local people and livestock.

Combining lemon balm with valerian in a tea and consuming before bed will also work to induce a restful night's sleep. Drinking lemon balm tea immediately after a meal can also help to improve digestion. Used in aromatherapy, lemon balm can aid relaxation, improve concentration, and lift the mood. To use it for this purpose, carry a bottle of pure lemon balm essential oil with you, smelling it regularly when needed, or burn the oil in an oil burner.

MARJORAM
Origanum majorana

Similar to oregano, marjoram is an aromatic herb that is part of the mint family. Native to the Mediterranean and western Asia, marjoram is a bushy plant with slightly oval-shaped leaves that grow in pairs along a square stem, and are sweet with a hint of citrus and pine. At the top of the stems, small white, purple, pink flowers bloom that have a similar appearance to hops.

The ancient Egyptians thought marjoram sacred to the god of the Underworld, Osiris, and because of this association, it was used as a funerary herb to embalm the bodies of the dead. In Greek mythology, marjoram was sacred to the god Hymen, the son of Aphrodite, and in ancient Rome, it was believed that the goddess of love Venus created the herb and gave it its sweet flavour. Due to this, it was thought to be a symbol of love, happiness, and joy as well as an aphrodisiac, and wreaths of marjoram were worn by young couples on their wedding day as a symbol of love and honor. This practice remained common throughout Europe during the Middle Ages.

Marjoram appears in *Banckes's Herbal*, the first herbal book printed in England in 1527, where it was noted for its sedative effects. A few centuries later, marjoram was found to have a narcotic effect when consumed in large amounts and, because of this, was included in the original recipe for absinthe when it was first introduced to France in the 1800s.

MAGICKAL PROPERTIES

Marjoram is associated with love and can be used in a wide range of love spells and rituals. It is believed that if you place dried marjoram in the four corners of your bedroom and under your pillow, you will dream about your future lover and attract them toward you. Another way to attract love toward you is to wear marjoram essential oil mixed with a carrier oil. To make, add 4 drops of essential oil to 0.3 fl oz (10 ml) of carrier oil, such as grapeseed or jojoba oil.

Drinking a cup of marjoram tea before any form of love divination can help you to clearly read any messages that come through during divining. If you use a pendulum, crystal ball, or runes, you can further increase the clarity of information that comes from your love reading by washing these divination tools in an infusion of marjoram before use. You can also use marjoram to help heal rifts and mend arguments within romantic relationships by sprinkling some

ZODIAC SIGNS
Gemini and Capricorn

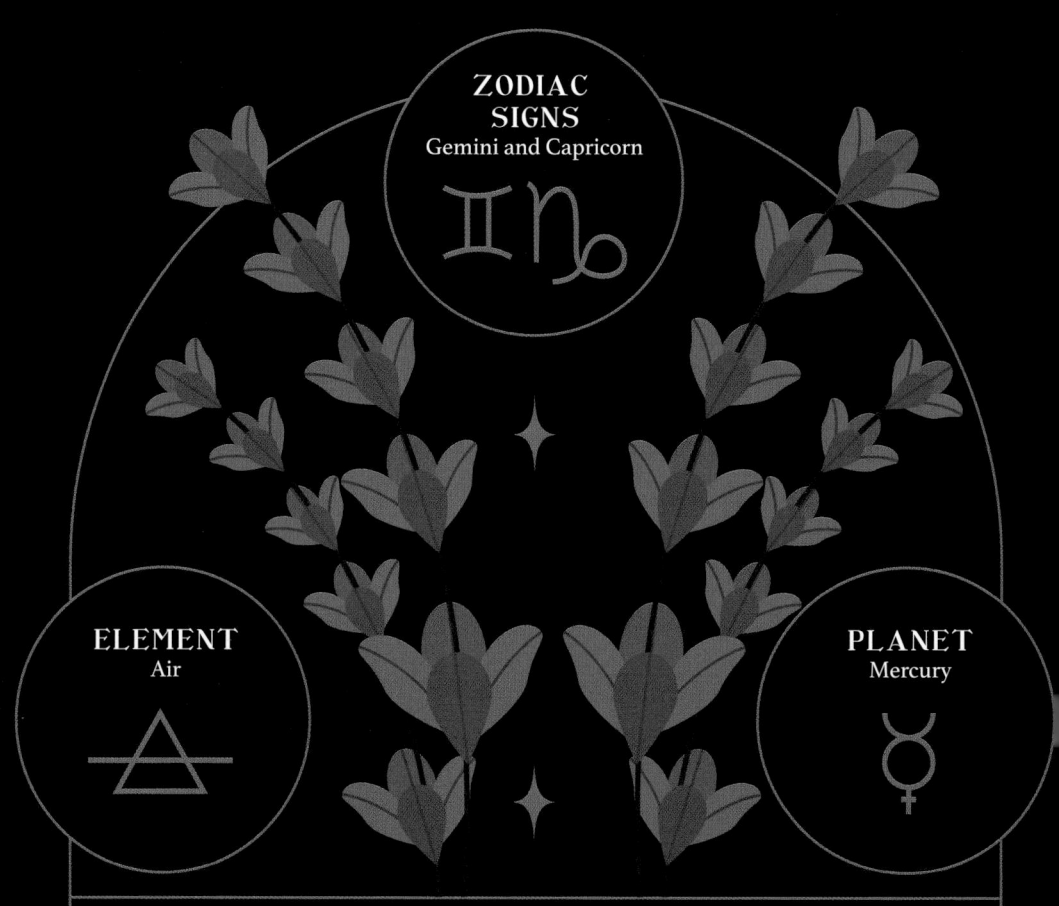

ELEMENT
Air

PLANET
Mercury

MARJORAM
Origanum majorana

MAGICKAL PROPERTIES
- Attracts love and dreams about your future lover
- Increases clear messages when divining
- Heals rifts and arguments
- Strengthens love
- Releases grief
- Brings happiness
- Removes negative energies

MEDICINAL PROPERTIES
- Eases digestive problems
- Relieves menstrual cramps
- Regulates hormones
- Relieves prementstual tension
- Calms nerves
- Eases emotional upset
- Reduces anxiety
- Helps insomnia

FOLK NAMES
Joy of the Mountain, Knotted Marjorane, Marjorlaine, Mountain Mint, Port Marjoram, Sweet Marjoram, Wintersweet

dried marjoram into your food, and sharing it with your lover. Marjoram's power to strengthen love can be further utilized by steeping 3 tsp of marjoram in 10 fl oz (300 ml) red or white wine for a few hours, and then sharing it with your partner to strengthen the love between you. Drinking marjoram in wine in this way can also help to release grief, bring happiness, and banish sadness.

Marjoram is highly protective. To protect your home or business, place dried marjoram leaves in the four corners of your house or business premises, replacing them every month. Dried marjoram can also be sprinkled around your business and home to draw in good fortune and remove any negative or harmful energies. For personal protection, you can place marjoram leaves in your pocket; just ensure you replace them every month in order to make sure they retain their power.

MEDICINAL PROPERTIES

Used in Mediterranean cooking, marjoram has a range of medicinal qualities. It can help digestive conditions as it relaxes the muscles within the digestive system to bring ease to stomach aches and pains and also indigestion. To help with these aliments, drink marjoram tea 3 times a day after meals. Marjoram also relaxes the muscles within the reproductive system to relieve menstrual cramps, and because it's able to regulate hormones, it can also bring relief from the symptoms of pre-menstrual tension. For this purpose, drink it as tea, or take as a syrup or tincture. To treat cramps, you can also add 6 drops of marjoram essential oil to a hot bath.

Marjoram helps to calm nerves and emotional upset. To make a tincture for this purpose, loosely fill an airtight jar with chopped-up marjoram, lemon balm, and lavender, then pour in enough 40% proof alcohol to cover all the plant matter. Seal the jar and store in a cool, dark place for 6 weeks, shaking daily. After this time, drain away the herbs and your tincture is ready to use. If you want to increase the potency, add fresh marjoram, lavender, and lemon balm and repeat the process. Take 20–50 drops of the tincture in total throughout the day to calm the nerves and emotions. This tincture can also ease insomnia and anxiety.

DISCLAIMER:
Do not use marjoram during pregnancy.

MINT
Mentha

FOLKLORE

Mint is an aromatic herb that grows fast and spreads easily if not tended to regularly. It has oval, jagged-edged, blunt-tipped leaves, and small purple, pink, and white flowers. Mint is usually harvested before it flowers as this improves the flavor of the leaves. There are 25 species in the mint family, which are native to Europe, Asia, North America, southern Africa, and Australia, although mint is spread throughout all temperate areas of the world.

In ancient Greek mythology, the genus Mentha is derived from Minthe, the name of a river nymph adored by the Greek god Hades (also known as Pluto). Hades' wife Persephone was jealous that his eyes had strayed, so she took her revenge by turning Minthe into the ground-growing plant we now know as mint so that everyone would walk over her for eternity. Hades tried to save Minthe, but was unable to undo the spell. Instead, he gave Minthe an aromatic fragrance that was released into the air when her leaves were stepped on or crushed.

Nicholas Culpeper in *Complete Herbal* wrote that mint shouldn't be given to a wounded person as it would stop their wounds healing. He also wrote that mint would "stir up venery or bodily lust", which is exactly why the ancient Greeks warned soldiers against using it. They believed that the increase in lust would lead to more lovemaking, which would diminish the courage a soldier needed on the battlefield. The ancient Romans, however, had a different view of mint. The Roman naturalist Pliny argued that mint was "contrary to procreation" and shouldn't be used by those wishing to conceive. He did, however, believe mint enhanced memory, so encouraged scholars to wear mint as crowns.

MAGICKAL PROPERTIES

Mint is known for its ability to attract abundance and prosperity. It's a great herb to include in prosperity bowls and to place in your wallet, along with money and your bank cards in order to bring prosperity and wealth into your life. For a simple prosperity candle spell, scratch the word "prosperity" into a green candle then dress the candle with mint and basil. Let the candle

ZODIAC SIGNS
Taurus and Virgo

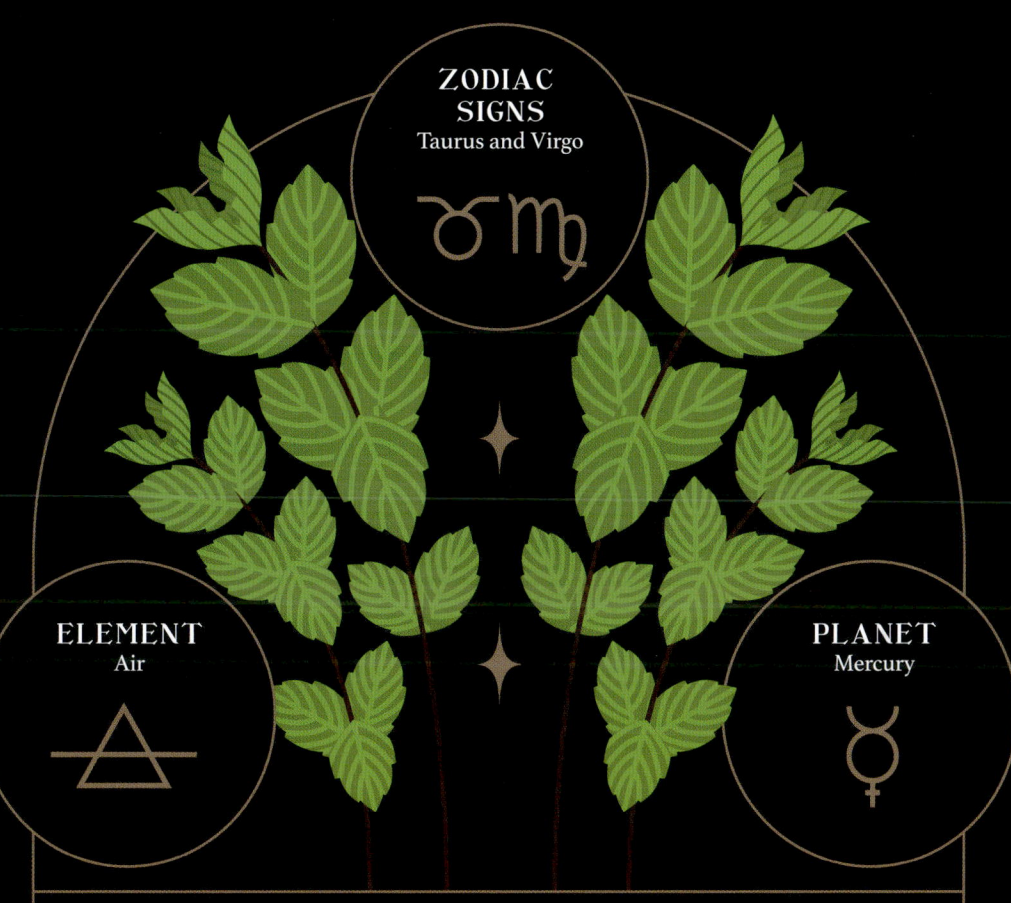

ELEMENT
Air

PLANET
Mercury

MINT
Mentha

MAGICKAL PROPERTIES
- Attracts money, prosperity, and abundance
- Purifies
- Protects
- Brings clarity of mind, renewal, and strength
- Welcomes new beginnings

MEDICINAL PROPERTIES
- Eases headaches
- Improves brain function
- Enhances memory
- Increases alertness
- Boosts concentration and focus
- Eases joint and muscle soreness
- Eases stomach pain
- Helps indigestion
- Eases irritable bowel syndrome

FOLK NAMES Garden Mint

burn out and bury the remnants in your yard to attract the prosperity you seek into your life.

Mint is a purifying herb that can be burned to clear away any negative energy from a space. It's a perfect herb to burn in order to purify ritual tools, and can be used after spell work to remove any residual energies from your work space. In folklore, mint is also used in exorcisms. As well as banishing, mint can attract and raise positive energies and good luck. Carry mint in a pouch or place a drop of mint essential oil on the tags in your clothes when you need a boost of luck.

Due to its protective qualities, mint can be used in any kind of protection spell or ritual as it stops any kind of negative and unwanted energy from interfering with your magick. Mint can also be used for home protection by placing a bowl of the herb by the entrance to your home, or by sprinkling it on the threshold.

This herb can also help you to find clarity of mind. If you're struggling to make a decision, hold 2–3 mint leaves in your hands when meditating and smell their aroma to receive the clarity of mind you need. Mint is also associated with renewal and strength and can be drunk as tea for this purpose. Using a handful of fresh mint leaves, this tea is also a good way to welcome in new beginnings.

MEDICINAL PROPERTIES

Mint is known for its ability to ease headaches. Mix 4 drops of mint essential oil to 0.3 fl oz (10 ml) of carrier oil and then rub it on your temples. Mint can also improve brain function when burned in essential oil form for when you're in need of an extra boost to memory. Smelling mint's aromatic fragrance can increase alertness, reduce frustration, and help the brain to retain information, particularly when studying. Burn mint essential oil in an oil burner or simply smell the essential oil from the bottle when you need it to boost your memory, concentration, and focus.

Mint can help to ease joint and muscle soreness and is a potent anti-inflammatory. Mix a few drops of mint essential oil in your hot bath water, or mix essential oil with carrier oil and massage onto the affected area to reduce soreness and pain.

Drinking mint in a tea can also ease a range of gastrointestinal conditions such as stomach pain, indigestion, and irritable bowel syndrome. Drinking a cup of mint tea 3 times a day made from a handful of fresh mint leaves works to regulate muscle relaxation, and helps reduce any gastrointestinal tract inflammation.

MUGWORT
Artemisia vulgaris

FOLKLORE

Native to Europe, Asia, and north Africa, mugwort can be considered an invasive weed. It has a reddish-brown stem, hairless dark green leaves that have a downy, slightly silvery underside, and reddish-green yellow flowers that grow in pinnacles with a distinct aroma. Mugwort is known as "the Witch's herb." The Latin name for mugwort is *Artemisia*, which is named after the Greek lunar goddess Artemis. She was the goddess of childbirth and midwives and protected young girls up until the age of marriage, which is why mugwort was often planted near the front door of the local healer, midwife, or Witch.

In the Middle Ages, mugwort was Christianized and became associated with John the Baptist rather than Artemis, where he carried the herb into the wilderness with him for protection. Due to this association, it became customary to wear a garland of mugwort on St John's day (June 24), which became known as "St John's Girdle" and would be thrown into a ceremonial fire to ensure protection for the year ahead. In the same period, it was believed that if mugwort was gathered on Midsummer's eve (as mugwort's powerful energies peaked at this time of year), it would protect against the plague and evil spirits. A Germanic folkloric practice also included digging underneath the roots of a mugwort plant to find coal, which could then be carried as protection against Witchcraft.

MAGICKAL PROPERTIES

Mugwort is associated with psychic abilities. It can be burned with wormwood as an incense during divination, and a cup of mugwort tea can be drunk before divination to enhance psychic powers. Mugwort oil can also be used for this purpose. Leave 2 tsp mugwort to infuse in 8.5 fl oz (250 ml) of carrier oil such as jojoba for at least a month, then rub it on your Third Eye. This herb, along with wormwood, can be made into an infusion (see page 14) and used to wash divination tools such as pendulums and crystal balls, which will help to enhance your psychic energies. Mugwort is also a key ingredient in flying ointment and has real psychoactive effects when consumed or put on your skin, so use sparingly. Flying oils have been used by Witches in centuries past. Witch trial records show that in 1477, a Witch called Antoine Rose (also known as the Witch of Savoy) used a flying oil to rub on an 18-inch stick given to her by the Devil, which she used to fly to the Sabbat.

A recipe for a flying ointment includes 2 tsp each of mugwort, rosemary, bay leaves, and damiana, and 1 tsp of wormwood. Place these ingredient in 12 fl oz (350 ml) of carrier oil such as almond or jojoba, and leave to infuse for 4–5 weeks. Then drain away and discard the herbs, placing the oil in a double boiler or in a heat-proof bowl placed over a pan of water on a low heat. Add 1.5 oz (45 g) of beeswax and stir until the wax has melted. While the mixture is still hot, pour into an airtight jar and leave to harden. Anoint your Third Eye, wrists, and chakra points about 30 minutes before bed to encourage lucid dreaming.

Mugwort tea can also enhance prophetic and lucid dreaming. Before bed, drink a cup of tea made from 1 part mugwort, 2 parts lemon balm, 2 parts linden, and 1 part lavender, leaving to steep for 15 minutes before drinking. As it steeps, breathe in the fragrant vapor to encourage lucid dreaming. Sleeping on mugwort is also believed to banish nightmares.

MEDICINAL PROPERTIES

Mugwort is associated with female health and, when consumed in small doses in tincture or tea form, can cause gentle contractions of the uterus that can promote regular menstruation, and regulate menstrual flow. It can also be used to induce labor, which is why those planning to conceive, are pregnant, or are breastfeeding should not use mugwort in any form.

Mugwort has antibacterial and antifungal properties. Applying an oil (made from fresh mugwort and a carrier oil that has been left for 4–6 weeks to infuse) to a wound will help to fight bacteria and infection. Mugwort is one of the herbs in the *Nine Herbs Charm* (see page 106), recorded in history for its ability to fight poisons.

Mugwort is an anti-inflammatory that can be used to treat joint pain and inflammation in the form of a salve or poultice (see pages 22 and 28). It can be used as a digestive aid to treat constipation, bloating, and diarrhea by making a tea from the flowers, and drinking before or after meals.

DISCLAIMER:
Do not use mugwort when trying to conceive, during pregnancy, or while breastfeeding.

ZODIAC SIGNS
Taurus and Libra

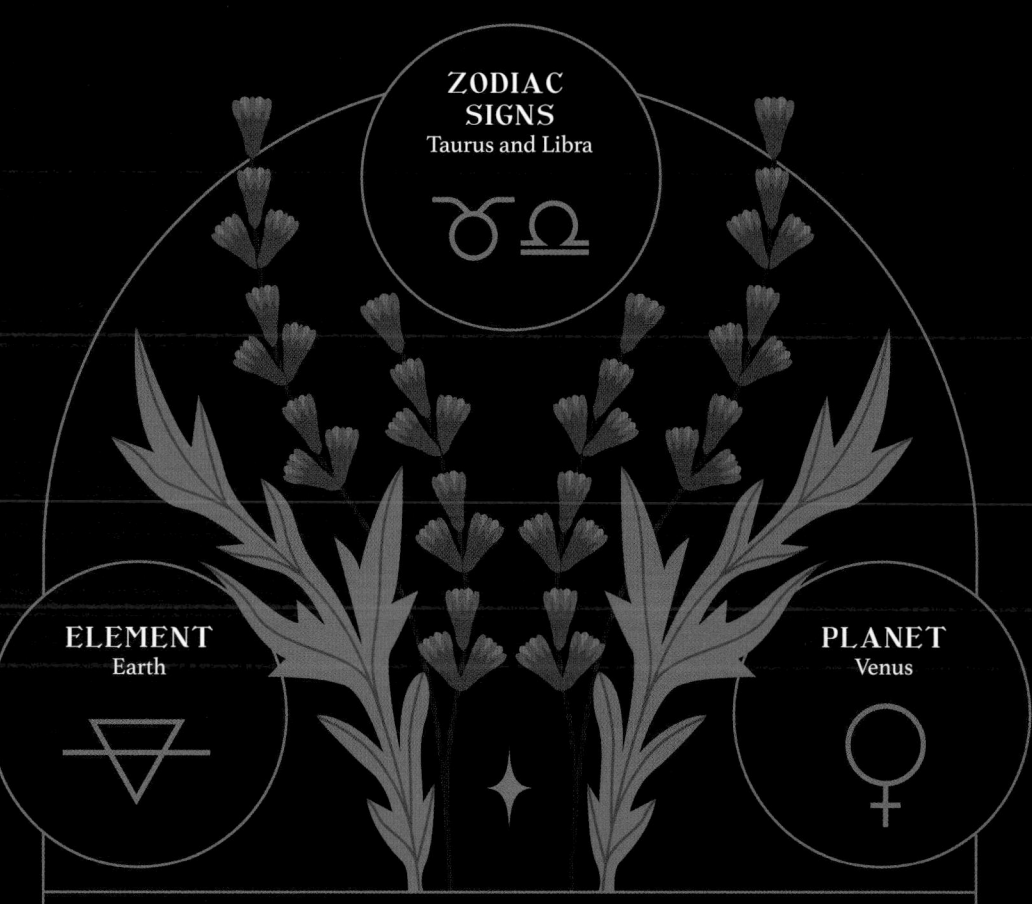

ELEMENT
Earth

PLANET
Venus

MUGWORT
Artemisia vulgaris

MAGICKAL PROPERTIES
- Enhances psychic abilities
- Enhances prophetic and lucid dreams
- Banishes nightmares
- Protects

MEDICINAL PROPERTIES
- Promotes regular menstruation
- Induces labor
- Fights poisons
- Reduces scarring
- Treats joint pain
- Fights constipation
- Relieves bloating and diarrhea
- Fights insomnia
- Reduces anxiety

FOLK NAMES
Artemisia, Cingulum Sancti, Felon Herb, Johannis, Maiden Wort, Mother's Wort, Mugger, Muggins, Muggons, Old Man, Old Uncle Harry, Sailor's Tobacco, Smotherwort, St John's Plant, Witches Herb

MULLEIN
Verbascum thapsus

FOLKLORE

Mullein has downy, velvety leaves that are larger and hairier at the base than at the tip. At the top are densely packed yellow flowers with five petals per flower. Native to Europe and Asia, mullein is considered a weed and can usually be found on wasteland, in fields, and by roadsides.

According to ancient Greek folklore, the gods gave Ulysses a stalk of mullein so he could defend himself against Circe, goddess of sorcery and daughter of the sun god Helios. During the medieval period, mullein was believed to protect against demons and black magick. It was also believed that Mary (the mother of Christ) would travel the land during harvest time to bless all the mullein, which is why it became known as "Our Lady's Candle." A popular rhyme at that time went, *"Our beloved Lady goes through the land, she carries mullein in her hand."*

The ancient Greeks and Romans, due to the height of a mature mullein plant, used it as a source of light. The Romans would dip mullein in tallow and set it alight, carrying it as a torch, particularly in funeral processions, which is why mullein is often associated with death. The Greeks would also use mullein to bring light, using the leaves to make into wicks that would be burned.

Known by one of its folk names, lungwort, mullein was known in the Roman times to be a cure for respiratory disease. An infusion or decoction would be made from the leaves, which would then be taken by humans and animals, as farmers gave them to their livestock to cure lung infections. In France, during the Middle Ages, farmers would also pass sprigs of mullein through the Midsummer ritual fire in order to protect their cattle from Witchcraft.

MAGICKAL PROPERTIES

Mullein is associated with protection and banishing negative energy. It can be used to smoke-cleanse your altar or the space where you perform spells and rituals to remove any unwanted or negative energy that may interfere with your magick. Mullein leaves can also be placed in a bag and then hung outside your home to protect your house from negative

ZODIAC SIGN
Leo
♌

ELEMENT
Fire
△

PLANET
Saturn
♄

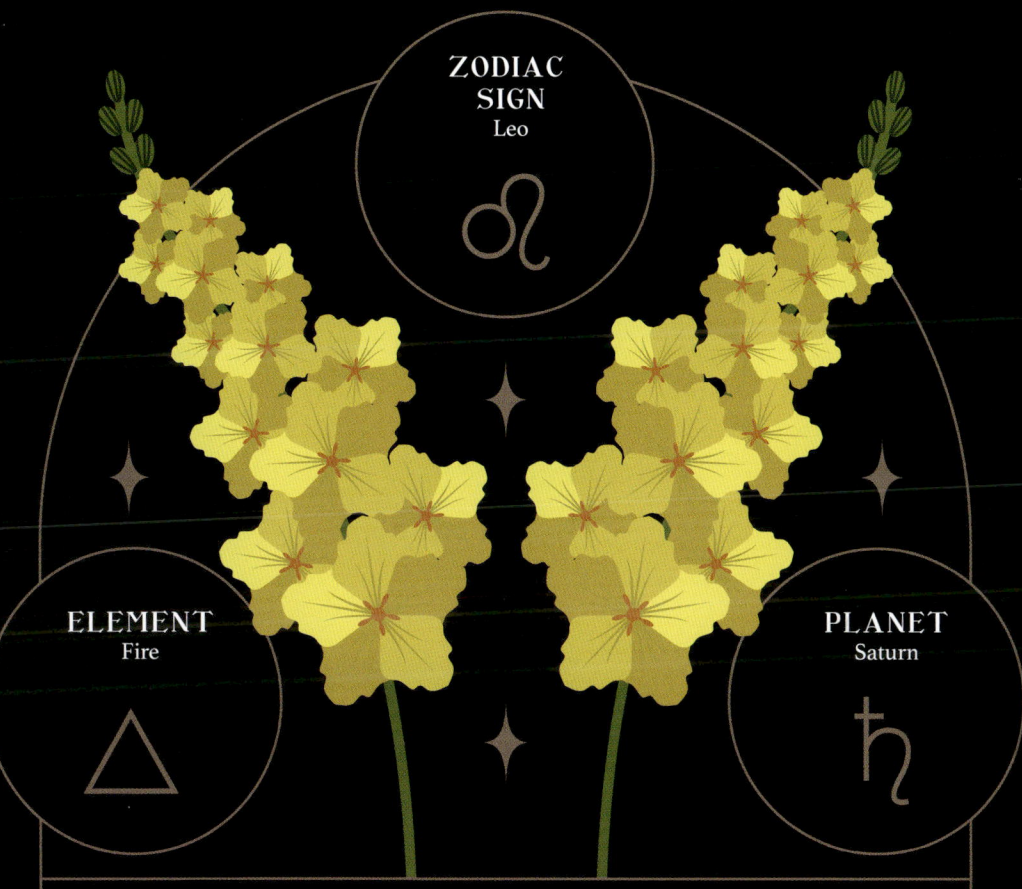

MULLEIN
Verbascum thapsus

MAGICKAL PROPERTIES
- Banishes negative energy
- Protects against nightmares
- Boosts courage
- Draws love from opposite sex
- Brings illumination
- Enhances understanding

MEDICINAL PROPERTIES
- Soothes eczema
- Improves respiratory health
- Treats coughs, colds, and flu
- Soothes burns

FOLK NAMES Aaron's Rod, Candlewick Plant, Clown's Lung-Wort, Flannel Plant, Great Mullein, Hag's Taper, Jacob's Staff, Our Lady's Flannel, Torches, Velvet Dock, Velvet Plant

energy entering it. Placing mullein leaves underneath your pillow can also protect against nightmares.

In magickal terms, mullein is associated with courage and can be used in a variety of ways. Drinking a tea made from the flowers and leaves can give you a boost of courage whenever needed. You can also wear the flowers as an amulet, or place them in your shoe to bring personal protection and increase courage when you're facing a difficult situation.

Mullein can draw love from the opposite sex and has a history of use in men's love magick. It can be carried in a pouch to gain the love of another. Burning mullein candles can help to bring illumination into your life and increase your understanding of an issue, as well as burned as part of funerary rites and remembering those who have passed. To make a mullein candle, dip a dried mullein stalk in candle wax, fully, 5–6 times, leaving each coat to completely cool before you apply the next. Once all the coats have been added and have completely hardened, pinch a small amount of wax off the end to make a wick before lighting. Due to its association with death, mullein can also be a substitute for graveyard dirt, which is used in folk magick for curses and necromancy.

MEDICINAL PROPERTIES

Mullein can be used to treat skin and soothe conditions like eczema. A hot oil infusion can be made and applied directly onto the affected area. Place a carrier oil such as almond or grapeseed oil in a double boiler or a heat-proof bowl over a pan of water along with mullein leaves and flowers, and gently heat for 3–4 hours. After this time, strain out the plant matter and your oil is ready to use. Due to mullein's anti-inflammatory properties, this oil can also be rubbed onto inflamed muscles and joints to help ease pain.

Like its folkloric use, mullein can be used to improve respiratory health and is a good expectorant, which can alleviate the symptoms of coughs, bronchitis, colds, and flu. Place the leaves and flowers in a bowl of hot water, then put your head over the bowl with a towel over your head and inhale the steam. A tea can be made from the leaves by leaving the plant matter to brew in hot water for 15–20 minutes before consuming. Drink 2–3 times a day.

Mullein also possesses antiviral and antibacterial properties. Leave mullein to steep in water for 3–4 hours and use the water to disinfect wounds and can help to sooth burns. To treat viruses, a syrup can be made from mullein flowers and leaves (see page 27). Take 3–4 times a day for as long as the viral infection persists.

NETTLE
Urtica dioica

FOLKLORE

Considered a weed, nettle can be found worldwide, particularly in Europe, north Africa, and North America. The leaves are jagged, tapered at the ends and, just like the nettle's stems, they are covered with thousands of tiny hairs. These hairs contain formic acid, which is responsible for causing pain when you brush up against it. Nettles also bear small green, white, and purple flowers that point upward, clustered between the leaf and stalk.

In Celtic folklore, groups of nettles indicate that faeries are living close by. The sting of a nettle was believed to protect against faerie mischief and also black magick. In Norse folklore, nettles were associated with Thor and Loki and it was believed that Loki made a fishing net made from nettle yarn so he could catch salmon. Nettles are also one of the "Nine Herbs Charm," which was a cure for infection and fought against poison (see page 106).

Nettles also have an important place in Romanian folklore. It is associated with the god of war Mars and was used for its protective qualities. It was eaten as part of a sacred meal at special times of the year such as during spring and Holy Week (the seven days prior to Easter Sunday). Nettles were also picked by young girls early in the morning on May 1 (Beltane) where they were boiled and then the water was used to rinse their hair to make it stronger.

The Anglo-Saxons considered nettle a sacred herb and nettle beer was drunk to alleviate rheumatism. The Native Americans also believed nettle would help to reduce joint pain and would purposely sting themselves as part of a ceremonial ritual to bring relief. The ancient Romans would also use nettle to ease pain; soldiers would carry the leaves to ease leg aches and pains from long journeys.

MAGICKAL PROPERTIES

Due to its forbidding appearance and its ability to sting, nettles are used for protection. They can be carried in a pouch or worn as an amulet for personal protection, scattered around the outside of your house to ward off evil, or burned as protective incense. Nettles can also be used to

ZODIAC SIGN
Aries

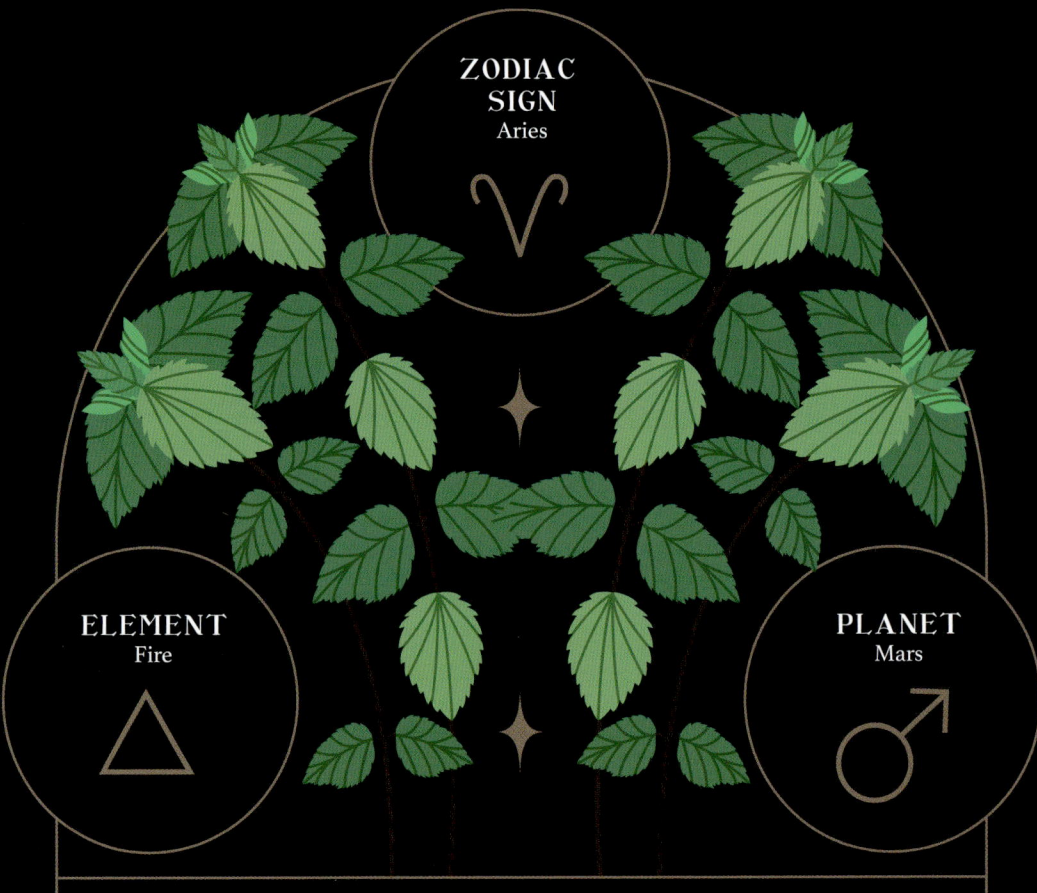

ELEMENT
Fire

PLANET
Mars

NETTLE
Urtica dioica

MAGICKAL PROPERTIES
- Protects
- Removes hexes and curses
- Wards off evil
- Promotes well-being
- Boosts strength and courage
- Purifies

MEDICINAL PROPERTIES
- Treats lower back pain
- Helps arthritic joints
- Treats eczema and acne
- Regulates hormonal imbalance
- Relieves menstrual cramps and heavy bleeding
- Treats urinary tract infections

FOLK NAMES Burn Hazel, Ortiga Ancha, Stinging Nettle

remove or protect from hexes; if you feel like you've been hexed, carry a poppet full of nettle leaves until the hex is removed. It can also be used to return the hex to its sender, so is a great herb to use in return to sender spells.

Nettles are associated with strength. Making a nettle tincture and taking 20–50 drops per day will help to increase your personal strength (see page 20). For a simple candle spell, dress a red candle with dried nettle and burn it for a boost of strength and courage. Once burned out, bury the remnants on your property to allow the continued flow of strength into your life.

Nettle also has the ability to cleanse and purify and is a great herb to burn before a spell or ritual to cleanse your work space. You can harness its cleansing properties by drinking nettle tea 3 times a day made from 6–8 nettle leaves. This will not only cleanse your energies but will also help to cleanse the body, bringing it back into balance with itself to promote feelings of well-being.

MEDICINAL PROPERTIES

Nettle has anti-inflammatory properties and is used to treat lower back pain and arthritis. To make a balm for this purpose, use 2 tbsp of dried nettle leaf, 2 tbsp of green nettle seed, and 6 fl oz (175 ml) of almond oil, leaving them to infuse in a sunny place for 3 weeks. After this time, place the strained oil in a double boiler or in a heat-proof bowl over a pan of water on a low heat, adding 0.5 oz (20 g) of beeswax, stirring until the wax melts. Pour into a jar and leave to set. Rub this balm onto the lower back and arthritic joints to help reduce pain and inflammation. Due to its anti-inflammatory and antimicrobial properties, making a nettle infusion to wash your face with daily can be an effective treatment for eczema and acne (see page 14).

Nettles can be used to elevate menstrual issues. Prepare nettle tea or soup and consume it a few days before menstruation begins and for the length of your period as it can regulate hormonal imbalances, reducing symptoms of premenstrual tension and aiding with menstrual cramps and heavy bleeding. Drinking nettle tea can also help relieve urinary tract infections as it can help to flush out the harmful bacteria. Drink 3 cups of tea each day.

Nettle is also excellent for when you are recovering from any kind of illness. It can be burned as incense in the room you are convalescing to help cleanse the body and promote healing, and a jar of fresh nettles can be placed next to the bed of the person who is sick to aid their recovery.

OREGANO
Origanum vulgare

FOLKLORE

Part of the mint family, oregano is a small evergreen shrub with oval leaves. The leaves and stem are covered in small hairs and it bares small white, pink, and purple flowers. Oregano is native to Mediterranean countries and west Asia, but is now also found in parts of Mexico and North America.

The ancient Romans believed the goddess of love, Venus, created oregano so that humans would always be reminded of her beauty due to its fragrance. The ancient Greeks, however, believed oregano was sacred to the goddess of love, Aphrodite. Oregano in Greek means "joy of the mountains" because it was said Aphrodite grew it on Mount Olympus as a symbol of happiness and joy. Due to these associations, the Greeks would also grow oregano on the graves of the dead to symbolize their happiness in the afterlife. Oregano is used at Samhain to ensure the happiness of loved ones who have passed.

Oregano is a common herb to use in all kinds of love spells. In European folklore, oregano was placed under an unmarried woman's pillow at night to help her dream of her future husband. On St Luke's Day, oregano was mixed with vinegar, honey, thyme, wormwood, and marigold, and was used to anoint a girl before bed so she could see her future spouse in her dreams. The Greeks and Romans would crown married couples with wreaths of oregano to ensure a happy marriage.

The Greek philosopher Aristotle believed that oregano was an antidote to poison. He believed, if eaten, oregano would also protect a person from being poisoned. This belief was prevalent in the Middle Ages where kings across Europe would eat oregano in their food everyday so they were protected from any assassination attempt by poison.

MAGICKAL PROPERTIES

Oregano is associated with love. It can be used to attract new love by wearing oregano oil on your pulse points or in your hair, or by carrying oregano in a pouch so that its sweet fragrance can be smelled. Oregano can be placed under your pillow to help conjure psychic dreams,

ZODIAC SIGNS
Taurus and Libra

ELEMENT
Air

PLANET
Mercury

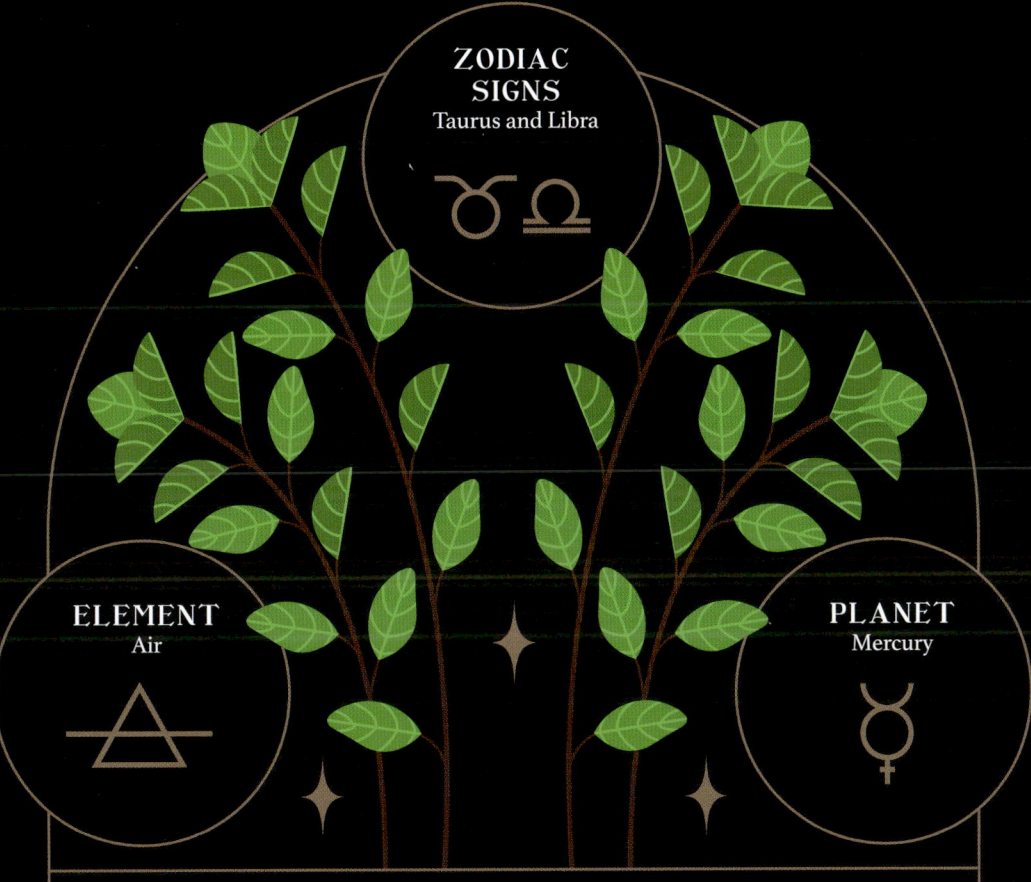

OREGANO
Origanum vulgare

MAGICKAL PROPERTIES
- Attracts love
- Increases psychic dreams
- Deepens existing love
- Brings happiness
- Increases courage
- Aids in letting go

MEDICINAL PROPERTIES
- Slows down the ageing process
- Reduces inflammation
- Relieves pain
- Disinfects wounds

FOLK NAMES Bastard Majoram, Joy of the Mountain, Rigani, Wild Majoram

particularly about your future lover. Before bed, take a purple candle and dress it with oregano, wormwood, and thyme, and burn it in your bedroom (but never go to sleep and leave the burning candle unattended) while focusing on the flame. When you feel ready, blow out the candle and go to sleep. Burn the candle whenever you want to induce psychic dreams.

Oregano can also deepen existing love by placing 2 tsp oregano in 8.5 fl oz (250 ml) red or white wine for 2–3 hours and then sharing it with your partner. Oregano is also a bringer of happiness. It can be placed in bags or bowls around your house or burned as incense to create a happy home environment. It can also be grown near the front door of your house to ensure that everyone that walks in will smell its sweet aroma and bring happiness into your home.

Oregano is associated with courage and with letting go. Draw a hot bath and add dried or fresh oregano leaves to the water and take a ritual bath to help increase courage when facing any challenges. This will also help you let go of the things in your life that no longer serve you.

MEDICINAL PROPERTIES

Oregano is packed with antioxidants, which protect the body against free radicals that play a significant role in the ageing process as well as causing some cancers.

Oregano has the power to reduce inflammation. A mixture of 4 tsp of dried oregano and 4 tsp of dried thyme can be diluted in 7 fl oz (200 ml) of light carrier oil such as jojoba or grapeseed, and rubbed into the affected area. The oil must be very concentrated for this purpose, so leave the herbs in the oil in an airtight jar for 4 weeks to infuse. After this time, drain the plant matter and add more oregano and thyme, leaving for another 4 weeks. After this time, repeat the process and after a month, drain the herbs using a strainer or cheesecloth. Your oil is now ready to use.

Oregano also has potent antibacterial properties that can help block the growth of certain bacteria that lead to infection. A poultice of oregano, thyme, and sage can be placed on wounds to keep them clean and stop them from getting infected (see page 28). A mix of these herbs can also be made into an infusion and be used to wash wounds to keep them infection free (see page 14).

PARSLEY
Petroselinum crispum

FOLKLORE

A herb of the carrot family, parsley is native to the Mediterranean. It's an aromatic plant with light green, hollow stems, and dark green curled leaves, which, on its second year of growth, produces small, yellow flowers. It can reach 12–39 in (30–100 cm) in height depending on the variety.

To the ancient Greeks, parsley was associated with death, as it was believed that it was formed from the blood of Archemorus whose name in Greek meant "the forerunner of death." When someone was gravely ill, the Greeks had a saying that they were "in need of parsley," which meant they were not expected to survive. They also placed parsley on graves, believing that it would reduce the smell of the corpse as it decomposed.

The Romans were thought to be the first to use parsley as a garnish, using it to freshen their breath after eating and to protect their food from contamination. They consumed it in large quantities as they also believed it would protect against intoxication.

In Medieval Europe, parsley was considered to be the Devil's herb, so to counteract this association, only women would sow parsley on Good Friday at 3 pm, the time of Christ's crucifixion, to banish the Devil's influence. Sowing the seeds when church bells rang made God's power over the Devil's herb stronger. It was believed that if the seeds didn't germinate, it was because the Devil's power was still strong or that the seeds were sown by a man.

MAGICKAL PROPERTIES

Parsley's folkloric connections to death makes it a powerful herb to use when communicating with the spirit world. It can enhance the ability to communicate with those who have passed and can be used in rituals honoring the dead, and when connecting with ancestors. Use fresh parsley to decorate your Samhain altar or burn dried parsley with mugwort and yarrow as incense when doing spirit work.

Centuries ago, it was dangerous to commune with spirits, as it was associated with the work of the Devil. The Crook of Devon Witch trials in 1662 is an example where 13 Witches, including Agnus Murie, Bessie Henderson, and Agnes Pittendreich were put to death for this spiritual practice.

Parsley is associated with protection and can ward off negative entities. Keep some parsley seeds on your altar to keep away negative energies or place them near the doors and windows of your home to stop any form of negativity from entering. A parsley oil can be made from the seeds and leaves by leaving them in a carrier oil such as almond or grapeseed for a month before using it to anoint yourself, your altar, and the doors of your home to create a shield against harmful influences.

Parsley is known for its association with love, passion, and lust, and has connections with fertility. Parsley can be worn as an amulet to attract love into your life, but make sure it's touching your skin. Carrying the seeds in a pouch can also increase fertility, not just if you're trying for a baby, but fertility in the form of the birth of new beginnings, ideas, and opportunities. Parsley can be chewed or put in a drink or food to share with your partner to increase the love between you.

MEDICINAL PROPERTIES

Parsley is rich in vitamin K, which is essential for bone health. Regularly consuming parsley in small amounts can help to support bone growth. Eating 10 small sprigs of parsley each day will give you the recommended daily amount of vitamin K to support bone density and reduce the risk of fractures.

Parsley is a natural diuretic and can help to support kidney health, although if you already have kidney troubles, parsley should not be consumed in large amounts. Taken as tea twice a day, parsley will help to keep kidneys healthy by removing any unwanted substances from your body, which can prevent and treat kidney stones.

Parsley is rich in carotenoids and vitamin A, which are needed to prevent eye disease and age-related eye degeneration. Half a cup of parsley each day can give you enough of the essential carotenoids and vitamins you need to support good eye health. This amount of parsley can be added to food, made into a tincture, brewed as tea, or taken in syrup form.

Parsley is also a purifier. Burn dried parsley with dried pine needles, common garden sage, and ethically sourced palo santo chips, and waft the smoke into all the corners of your home.

DISCLAIMER:
Parsley should not be eaten in large amounts by anyone with kidney troubles, on blood thinning medication, or those who are pregnant or breastfeeding.

ZODIAC SIGNS
Virgo, Cancer, and Libra

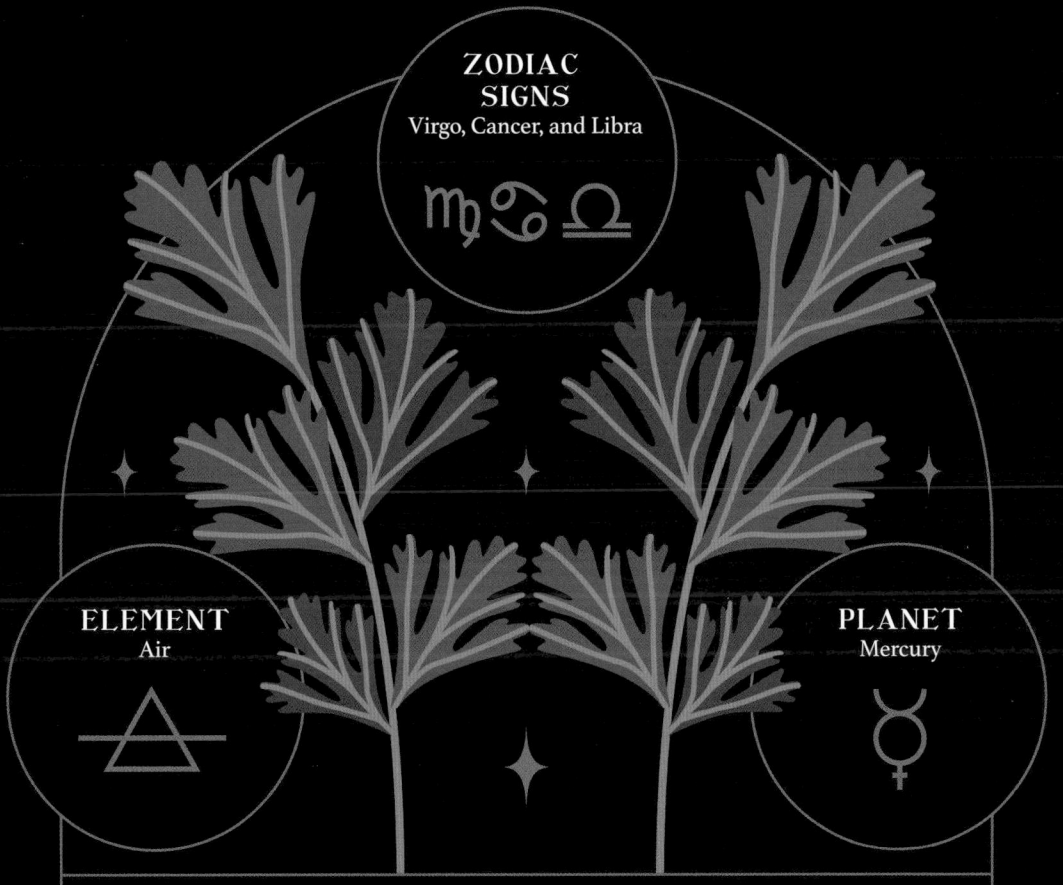

ELEMENT
Air

PLANET
Mercury

PARSLEY
Petroselinum crispum

MAGICKAL PROPERTIES
- Aids communication with the spirit world
- Honors the dead
- Protects
- Wards off negative entities
- Increases strength, love, passion, lust, and fertility

MEDICINAL PROPERTIES
- Aids bone health
- Protects against osteoporosis
- Keeps kidneys healthy
- Prevents kidney stones
- Clears urinary tract infections
- Reduces bloating and water retention
- Prevents eye disease

FOLK NAMES Devil's Oatmeal, Percely, Persil, Petersilie, Rock Parsley

PEPPERMINT
Mentha piperita

FOLKLORE

Peppermint is an aromatic herb and is a popular flavor in food, chewing gum, toothpaste, and cosmetic products. Native to Europe and the Middle East, it is now grown all over the world, and is a cross between spearmint and water mint. Peppermint has dark green, veiny, oblong shaped leaves that are jagged around the edges, and its light, delicate, lilac flowers bloom throughout the summer.

Peppermint has been used for thousands of years. In ancient Egypt, medical texts wrote about peppermint's ability to ease stomach issues, and in 1550 BC, the Egyptian "Ebers Papyrus" wrote about peppermint's ability to soothe digestive issues and treat flatulence. There is even archaeological evidence that mint leaves were found in the Egyptian pyramids at Giza. The ancient Greeks and Romans also used peppermint to soothe the stomach.

The oil extracted from the leaves was considered to be very valuable to the Egyptians, and was even traded as a form of money. It is from this time that the term "minting money" emerged, when peppermint was used as a form of currency. In St Luke's Gospel in the Bible, there is also mention of peppermint being used as a way to pay taxes.

Like mint, peppermint also has the same folklore attached to it that comes from the ancient Greeks. Persephone, the wife of Hades, turned the nymph Minthe, who had seduced Hades, into a mint plant as punishment so that she would be walked upon.

MAGICKAL PROPERTIES

Peppermint has a whole host of magickal properties. It is associated with prosperity and has the ability to draw money to you. Carry a pouch of peppermint along with basil to attract wealth toward you. For a simple candle spell, use dried peppermint and basil to dress a green candle and burn it to welcome prosperity and money into your life. Keep a peppermint leaf in your wallet to keep money flowing into your life. Peppermint is also associated with good luck. Anoint yourself with peppermint oil behind your ears or put some on the tags of your clothes

ZODIAC SIGNS
Gemini and Aries

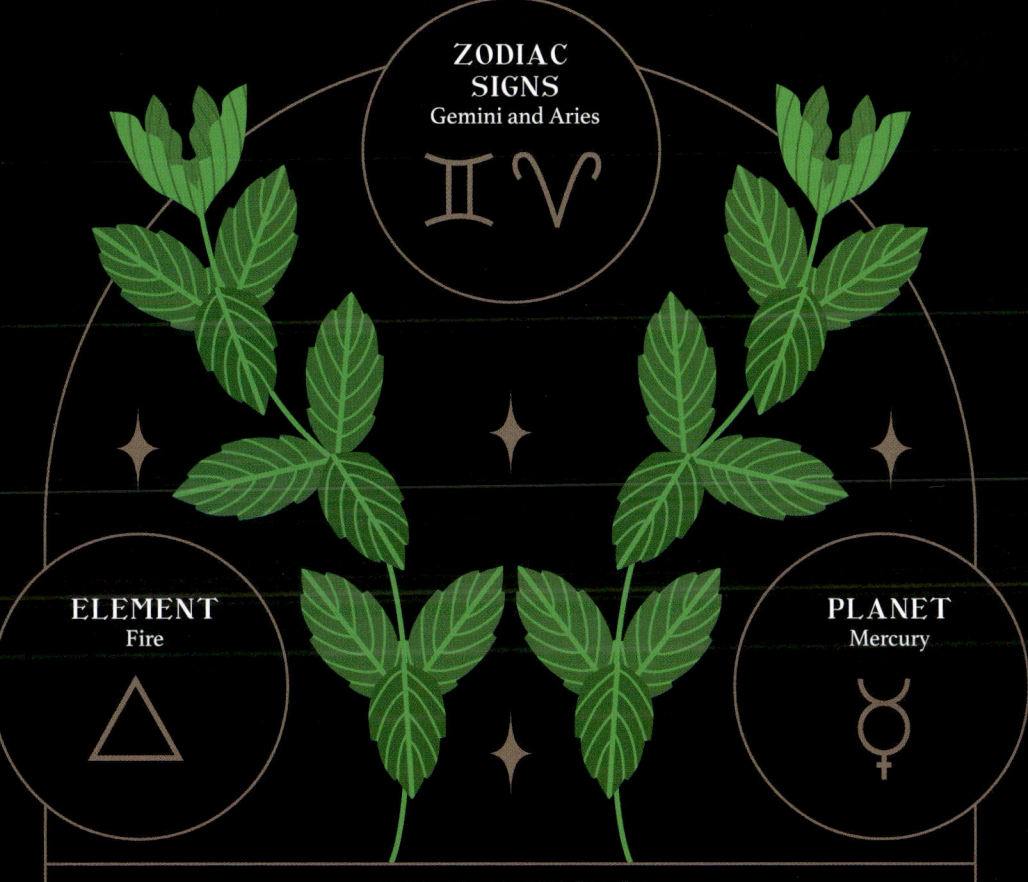

ELEMENT
Fire

PLANET
Mercury

PEPPERMINT
Mentha piperita

MAGICKAL PROPERTIES
- Attracts prosperity
- Draws money and wealth
- Brings good luck
- Cleanses and purifies
- Promotes restful sleep
- Awakens the Third Eye
- Brings mental clarity
- Attracts love
- Excites passion
- Increases sexual stamina

MEDICINAL PROPERTIES
- Soothes stomach ache
- Treats irritable bowel syndrome
- Alleviates digestive issues
- Reduces bloating
- Eases tension headaches
- Relieves pain
- Reduces migraines

FOLK NAMES Brandy Mint, Lanmint

when you are in a situation where you need a boost of luck.

Peppermint has cleansing and purifying qualities. Dried peppermint stems (with leaves) can be made into a bundle and burned to drive away negative energies, or can be put in hot water and used to wash the floors in your house. A tea made from a handful of fresh peppermint leaves and drunk 3 times a day can also be used to cleanse the body, andpeppermint tea drunk before bed can help to promote restful sleep and awaken the Third Eye. It can produce prophetic dreams, which makes it perfect to drink during divination as it enhances intuition.

Associated with clarity, peppermint has the ability to bring mental clarity. Carry peppermint with rosemary in a pouch in situations where you need clarity. These herbs can also be burned as incense, drunk as tea, or made into an oil and burned on an oil burner to clear the mind, and see things as they really are.

A popular herb to use in love spells, peppermint can excite passion. If you're looking for love, carry peppermint around with you in a pouch to attract the love you seek toward you. Fresh peppermint leaves can actually be chewed on in order to increase sexual stamina.

MEDICINAL PROPERTIES

Peppermint can be used for a variety of different conditions. It can help to ease digestive issues, nausea, and cramps, and can even soothe the stomach and irritable bowel syndrome as it helps to relax the colon. Make a tea using 2 tsp of the herb to about 8 fl oz (235 ml) of water, leaving it to steep for 15–20 minutes. Drink this after every meal to alleviate any bloating and any digestive problems or conditions. This tea can also help with tension headaches. For this purpose, take this tea twice a day for as long as headaches persist. A tincture can also be made using fresh peppermint. Add fresh peppermint to an airtight jar until it is ¾ full, then add 40% proof vodka until it completely covers the herbs. Leave in a dark, cool place for 6 weeks, shaking daily. After this time, it's ready to use. Take 20–50 drops of the tincture daily in three separate doses.

Peppermint can help to give pain relief. To use it for this purpose, make an oil using fresh peppermint leaves and a carrier oil such as jojoba or grapeseed. Combine in an airtight jar, and leave for 4–6 weeks (shaking daily). Rub onto the painful area to reduce sensitivity to pain. Smelling a bottle of peppermint essential oil can bring relief to migraines, as can mixing 10 drops of peppermint essential oil with 8.5 fl oz (250 ml) of a carrier oil such as sunflower or jojoba, and rubbing it on the temples.

ROSEMARY
Rosmarinus officinalis

FOLKLORE

Part of the mint family, rosemary is native to the Mediterranean, although is now grown throughout Europe. It has needle-like leaves, which are dark green in color on the upper side, and silver-gray on the underside. Rosemary is a highly fragrant plant. Mature rosemary plants have purple and blue flowers growing at the ends of the stems.

The ancient Egyptians used rosemary as part of burial rituals, and archaeologists have found sprigs of rosemary in Egyptian tombs dating back to 3000 BC. The ancient Greeks believed that rosemary boosted the memory, which is why scholars often wore it on their heads during exams. This association between rosemary and memory can also be seen years later in Shakespeare's *Hamlet* when Ophelia states "There's rosemary, that's for remembrance."

Rosemary was believed to be a sign of love and fidelity. In Tudor England, Henry VIII's fourth wife, Anne of Cleves, wore rosemary in her hair at her wedding, and this tradition continued throughout the Victorian period, where brides placed rosemary in their bridal bouquets. This was also used as a reminder of the good memories they brought into the marriage and the memories the couple would make together in their new life.

The color of rosemary flowers became linked to the Virgin Mary. Folklore states that when Mary, Joseph, and Jesus fled to Egypt, Mary used a rosemary bush to dry her blue clothes, which turned the white flowers blue. From this point onward, the herb was known as "the rose of Mary."

MAGICKAL PROPERTIES

Rosemary was used in the 4th century to ward off the Black Death, and today, this herb is still known for its magickal cleansing and purifying properties. Tie a bundle of dried rosemary together and burn it as a form of smoke purification to remove any negative or unwanted energies. The dried leaves can also be burned on a charcoal disc or added to a ritual bath for the same purpose. Rosemary is known for its ability to boost the memory, and simply smelling the fragrance of rosemary essential oil from the bottle when studying or reading can help you to retain information. For best results, burn the rosemary essential oil in an oil burner and drink rosemary tea while completing any task where you want to increase your memory's capacity.

Rosemary can ward off evil spirits. Hang sprigs of dried rosemary in your home to stop unwanted energies entering, or carry rosemary in a pouch for personal protection.

This plant is also used in love spells and rituals. To attract romantic love into your life, fill a heart-shaped poppet with rosemary and keep it with you so you send out energies into the universe about the love you want to attract.

Rosemary can help to remove jealousy. Hold a sprig of the dried herb in your hand and visualize your jealous energies transferring to the rosemary. Once you feel ready, set the rosemary alight and visualize your jealousy disappearing as the herb burns. Once fully burned, take the ash and throw it into the wind to remove it from your life.

MEDICINAL PROPERTIES

Rosemary can be used to treat digestive issues, including heartburn and indigestion. Mix a few drops of rosemary essential oil with 1 tbsp of light carrier oil such as sunflower or grapeseed and use it to massage your stomach when experiencing any kind of digestive problems. Drinking rosemary tea before meals can also help to stimulate hunger and counteract a loss of appetite, as well as reduce gastric issues.

Due to its antibacterial properties, rosemary fights a number of bacterial infections. Make a tea from rosemary leaves and leave to steep for 15 minutes. Once cooled, you can use it to wash infected wounds 3 times a day, until the infection is gone. This tisane can be used to clean cuts and scrapes to prevent them from becoming infected.

Rosemary can be used to treat inflammation. An easy massage oil can be made from 6 drops of rosemary essential oil mixed with 1 tbsp of carrier oil such as jojoba or grapeseed and can be applied to any affected areas, such as muscles, joints, and sprains. This is also an effective treatment for arthritis and headaches. For a full body experience, put 6–7 drops of rosemary essential oil into a hot bath and soak in the water for at least 20 minutes.

DISCLAIMER:
Avoid using rosemary as anything other than a spice in cooking during pregnancy.

ZODIAC SIGNS
Leo and Aries

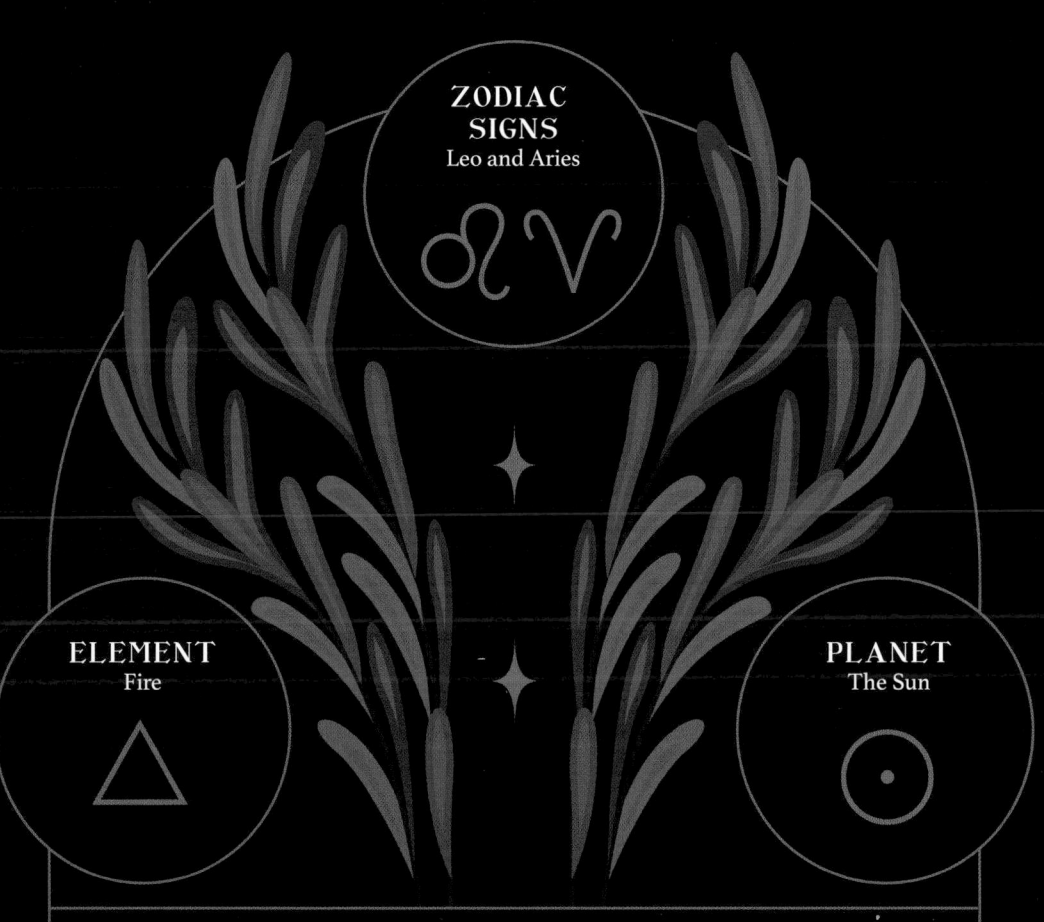

ELEMENT
Fire

PLANET
The Sun

ROSEMARY
Rosmarinus officinalis

MAGICKAL PROPERTIES
- Cleanses and purifies
- Boosts memory
- Increases capacity to retain information
- Protects
- Wards off evil spirits
- Attracts romantic love
- Removes jealousy

MEDICINAL PROPERTIES
- Treats heartburn
- Aids digestion
- Stimulates hunger
- Reduces gastric issues
- Treats spains
- Eases arthritic pain
- Soothes headaches

FOLK NAMES Compass Weed, Elf Leaf, Dew of the Sea, Guardrobe, Polar Plant

ZODIAC SIGNS
Aries and Capricorn

ELEMENT
Water

PLANET
Venus

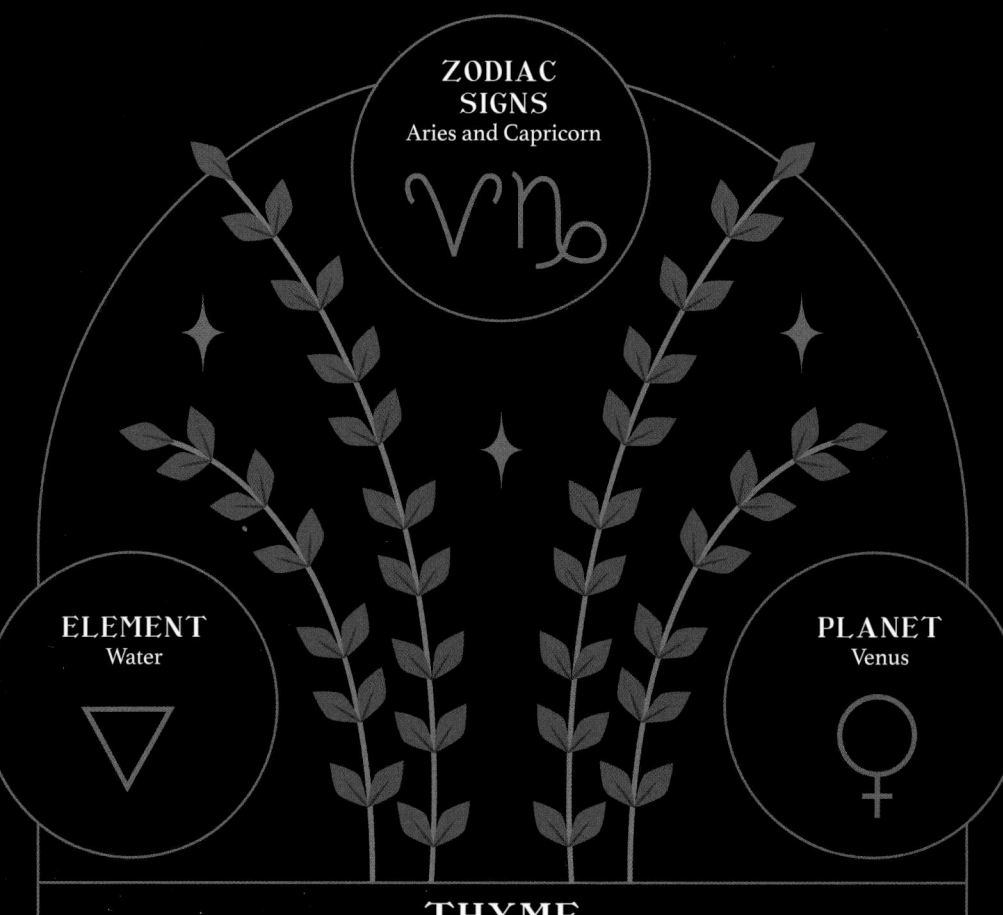

THYME
Thymus vulgaris

MAGICKAL PROPERTIES
- Purifies and cleanses
- Clears negative emotional energy
- Increases bravery
- Enhances confidence
- Gives courage
- Prevents nightmares
- Aids spirit work and ancestral communication

MEDICINAL PROPERTIES
- Disinfects
- Purifies the air of pollutants
- Treats coughs
- Boosts natural immunity
- Regulates mood

FOLK NAMES Common Thyme, Garden Thyme

THYME
Thymus vulgaris

FOLKLORE

Part of the mint family, thyme is a highly aromatic herb native to Eurasia. It has small gray-green oval leaves that grow along the woody stems, and when a thyme plant is mature, it is covered in tiny purple and white flowers throughout the summer.

The name thyme is believed to be derived from the Greek word *thumos*, meaning "smoke," as the ancient Greeks would burn it, using the fragrant smoke to purify their space. The word *thumos* can also mean bravery because the ancient Greeks considered thyme to be a symbol of courage. It would be carried by soldiers before going into battle for bravery and strength. This association spread throughout Europe during the Middle Ages, when ladies would embroider a bee on a sprig of thyme onto a piece of material, which they would give to a knight for courage.

Thyme was also considered a funerary herb and was used by the ancient Egyptians in funerary rites and rituals. It was believed that the souls of the dead could reside in a piece of thyme until it was time for their burial, after which the thyme would be buried with the body. It was also believed that it helped the living reconnect with their ancestors and the souls of their departed loved ones.

Thyme is also associated with many Biblical references. It was believed that the straw in the stable on which Mary gave birth to Jesus contained thyme among other herbs, and was often known as "Our Lady's bed-straw." In England, during the medieval period, thyme was also used as bedding, and mattresses were stuffed with the herb, as it was believed to ward off nightmares.

MAGICKAL PROPERTIES

As a fumigatory herb, thyme can be used to purify. Tie dried sprigs of thyme together and burn it to purify your altar before a spell or ritual to stop any unwanted energies from interfering with the energies of your spell. You can also use it to cleanse your home, or any kind of space, to remove negative energies. Burn dried thyme on a charcoal disc in the home to clear negative emotional energy, particularly after an argument or disagreement.

Thyme can enhance bravery. Before an event that requires confidence and courage, take a bath with 7 drops of thyme essential oil to increase your sense of boldness.

Thyme can prevent nightmares. During the 1600s, distilled thyme water with rose vinegar was taken before bed. A sprig of thyme placed under your pillow can ward off bad dreams.

Due to its association with ancestors, thyme can be used to aid spirit work. Drinking tea made from 3 tsp of dried thyme will help you to communicate with loved ones that have passed. In Cornish folklore, 1 tsp juniper, 3 tsp mugwort, 2.5 tsp myrrh, 1 tsp star anise, 2 tsp vervain, and 1.5 tsp wormwood were mixed with 12 drops of camphor oil and 7 drops of thyme oil to create crow smoke. This can be used to dress candles or be burned in an oil burner to aid with ancestral communication.

MEDICINAL PROPERTIES

Thyme is known for its disinfectant properties in the home, and can help to purify the air, particularly if there is mould in the house. Add 5 drops of thyme essential oil to a bucket of hot water and use it to clean wherever there is mould present. Using thyme oil in an oil burner afterward will help to fully cleanse the air of any residual pollutants.

Thyme is antibacterial and can be effective on antibiotic-resistant strains of bacteria. To make a thyme oil, place 2 tbsp of dried thyme in an airtight jar with 5 fl oz (150 ml) of olive oil, and leave to steep for 4 weeks. After this time, drain and discard the plant matter with a strainer or cheesecloth and then add another 2 tbsp of dried thyme into the oil. Shake daily. After another 4 weeks, the oil is ready to use. Take 1 tbsp of oil 3 times a day until the infection is gone. This oil is also useful for treating coughs and boosting natural immunity.

It has been shown in scientific studies that thyme helps to naturally boost dopamine and serotonin, which are crucial for regulating mood. Consuming thyme regularly, like in the form of the oil above, drinking a cup of thyme tea made from 4 tsp of dried thyme and brewed for 15 minutes, or making a thyme syrup (see page 27) and taking 1 tsp each day can always help to boost your mood.

VALERIAN
Valeriana officinalis

FOLKLORE

Valerian is a perennial plant that grows to 5–6 ft (1.5–1.8 m) tall, with branched clusters of pink or white sweet-smelling flowers. Valerian is native to Europe and Asia, but is naturalized to North America, growing in damp meadows, grasslands, and near streams.

In ancient Greece and Rome, Valerian was used to treat anxiety, insomnia, and headaches. According to folklore, the goddess Aphrodite was responsible for giving valerian to physician Claudius Galenus in order to treat insomnia, and it has been used ever since this time.

In Norse mythology, the goddess Freya was believed to create love potions containing valerian to make men fall in love with her. Much later in Europe, during the Middle Ages, valerian was used as a potent love charm that was believed to attract the opposite sex. This is why, in English folklore, valerian was believed to have aphrodisiac properties, and would be carried by young women who wanted to attract a lover. In Sweden, however, valerian was carried by a bridegroom at his wedding, not to attract love, but to ward off the jealousy of elves.

In the medieval period, valerian was also used in food and drink as a common flavoring agent, and during Anglo-Saxon times, the leaves and stems of this plant were a popular ingredient in salads.

Valerian was believed to attract cats and rats and the ancient Egyptians used valerian for this purpose, as cats were sacred to them. Valerian's ability to attract rats is also well known from the story of the Pied Piper of Hamelin, where the Piper carried valerian root in his back pocket in order to lure rats away from the city.

MAGICKAL PROPERTIES

Valerian is well known for its protective properties. The Celts believed valerian would protect against lightning strikes, and the ancient Greeks would hang bundles of the root in their homes near windows in order to protect against unwanted visitors and evil. Due to the strong smell of its roots, valerian is a good ingredient to use in a protective spell jar (along with rosemary, chamomile, nettles, and the rune Elhaz—also known as Algiz—drawn onto a small piece of paper). To prevent the odour from spreading around your home, use an airtight jar. Many Witches in centuries past used protective spell jars in their Craft. The 19th-century Irish Witch Biddy Early was famous for her blue-bottled protective spell jar, which she carried throughout her life.

This herb is associated with sleep and dream magick. In medieval English folklore, valerian root was placed under the pillow to protect against evil spirits and bad dreams. Alternatively, due to the strong smell of the valerian root, you can fill a mason jar with the root and place it under your bed for the same purpose. The root can also help to induce lucid dreaming by drinking a cup of valerian root tea or infusion 20 minutes before going to sleep.

Valerian is associated with love and attraction. Carry valerian in a pouch or make a valerian oil along with red rose petals, basil, and lavender, and rub it on your wrists to attract love into your life (see page 18). Burning incense made from dried valerian, cinnamon, nutmeg, ginger, and dried patchouli in your home will help to attract passionate, fiery love. In English folklore, a pouch of valerian was pinned to the clothes of a woman to attract the attentions of the opposite sex.

MEDICINAL PROPERTIES

Valerian roots have a strong earthy aroma, which is believed to be a sign of their medicinal power. The word valerian is derived from the Latin word *valere*, which means "to be strong and healthy," which explains why many healing herbal folkloric preparations contained it.

Throughout the centuries, valerian has been known for its ability to treat insomnia and anxiety, and for its sedative properties. A tea made by combining 2 tsp each of valerian root, passionflower, lavender, and skullcap, and leaving to brew for 5–7 minutes, can be drunk before bed to induce a restful night's sleep. To treat anxiety as well as insomnia, make a valerian root tincture by adding 4 tsp of valerian root to 8.5 fl oz (250 ml) of vodka, and leave to steep for 4 weeks. Take 15–20 drops with hot water or under the tongue 20 minutes before bed.

Classified by western herbalism as a nervine remedy, valerian works by encouraging muscles to relax. This makes it perfect to treat headaches, period pains, and muscle tension. A salve can be made using 2 tsp each of valerian, chamomile, turmeric, and willow bark; 9 fl oz (260 ml) of grapeseed oil; and 1 oz (30 g) of beeswax (see page 22). Rub it on the temples or wherever you feel any muscle tension.

ZODIAC SIGNS
Gemini, Libra, and Aquarius

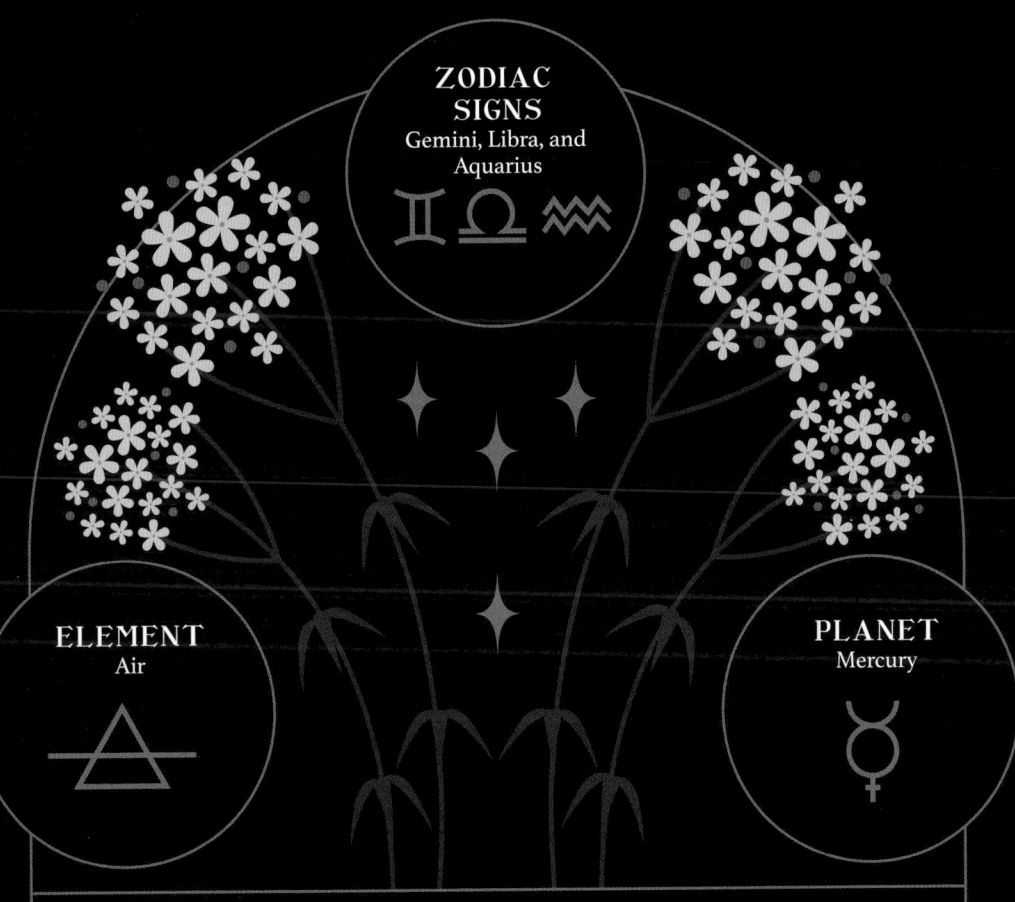

ELEMENT
Air

PLANET
Mercury

VALERIAN
Valeriana officinalis

MAGICKAL PROPERTIES
- Protects
- Aids sleep and dream magick
- Attracts love and affection
- Assists in shadow work magick
- Sedates
- Improves peace and serenity
- Stops arguments

MEDICINAL PROPERTIES
- Promotes restful sleep
- Treats insomnia
- Soothes nervous tension
- Balances nervous system
- Calms
- Helps tension headaches
- Treats menopause symptoms
- Treats premenstrual tension

FOLK NAMES
All Heal, Cats Paw, Great Wild Valerian, Moon Root, Phu, Setwall, Valerian, Valeriane

THE NINE HERBS CHARM

This is a 10th century Anglo-Saxon charm against infections and poison. It contains nine herbs: mugwort, buckthorn, lamb's cress, nettle, betony, chamomile, crab apple (flowers and leaves), chervil, and fennel. To make this charm, grind up the herbs while speaking the name of each. Then mix the herbs together as you say the words below. To treat infections, mix the herbs with wood or charcoal ashes and water to form a paste, applying to the affected area. To treat poison, mix in a drink and consume.

Remember, mugwort, what you made known,
What you arranged at the Great proclamation.
You were called Una, the oldest of herbs,
you have power against three and against thirty,
you have power against poison and against contagion,
you have power against the loathsome foe roving through the land.
And you, buckthorn, mother of herbs,
Open to the east, mighty inside.
Over you chariots creaked, over you queens rode,
over you brides cried out, over you bulls snorted.
You withstood all of them, you dashed against them.
May you likewise withstand poison and infection
and the loathsome foe roving through the land.
Lamb's cress is the name of this herb, it grew on a stone,
it stands up against poison, it dashes against pain,
Nettles it is called, it drives out the hostile one, it casts out poison.
This is the herb that fought against the snake,
it has power against poison, it has power against infection,
it has power against the loathsome foe roving through the land.
Put to flight now, betony, the greater poisons,
though you are the lesser,
you the mightier, conquer the lesser poisons, until he is cured of both.
Remember, chamomile, what you made known,
that never a man should lose his life from infection
after chamomile was prepared for his food.
This is the herb that is called crab apple
A seal sent it across the sea-right,

a vexation to poison, a help to others.
It stands against pain, it dashes against poison,
it has power against three and against thirty,
against the hand of a fiend and against mighty devices,
against the spell of mean creatures.
There the apple accomplished it against poison
that she the loathsome serpent would never dwell in the house.
Chervil and fennel, two very mighty one.
They were created by the wise Lord,
holy in heaven as He hung;
He set and sent them to the seven worlds,
to the wretched and the fortunate, as a help to all.
These nine have power against nine poisons.
A worm came crawling, it killed nothing.
For Woden took nine glory-twigs,
he smote the adder that it flew apart into nine parts.
Now these nine herbs have power against nine evil spirits,
against nine poisons and against nine infections:
Against the red poison, against the foul poison.
against the yellow poison, against the green poison,
against the black poison, against the blue poison,
against the brown poison, against the crimson poison.
Against worm-blister, against water-blister,
against thorn-blister, against thistle-blister,
against ice-blister, against poison-blister.
Against harmfulness of the air, against harmfulness of the ground,
against harmfulness of the sea.
If any poison comes flying from the east,
or any from the north, or any from the south,
or any from the west among the people.
Woden stood over diseases of every kind.
I alone know a running stream,
and the nine adders beware of it.
May all the weeds spring up from their roots,
the seas slip apart, all salt water,
when I blow this poison from you.

Avoid mugwort and betony if you are pregnant or breastfeeding. Note that buckthorn is a laxative.

Flowers

CARNATION
Dianthus caryophyllus

FOLKLORE

Originating from the Mediterranean, the Latin name for carnations, *Dianthus*, is attributed to the Greek botanist Theophrastus, and means "flower of the gods." In ancient Greek folklore, carnations were associated with the goddess Diana. She fell in love with a shepherd who did not reciprocate her feelings, so she gouged his eyes out and where blood fell on the ground, red carnations began to bloom. Similarly, in Christian lore, red carnations began to grow where the Virgin Mary's tears fell as she watched the crucifixion of Christ.

In Nordic tradition, carnations represent the promise of love. A bride would wear the flower on her clothes, which the bridegroom would later have to find after the wedding. Chinese mythology also associated carnations with long-lasting love, as well as good luck and happiness.

MAGICKAL PROPERTIES

Wearing a carnation can help to attract love, as can burning the petals of the flowers (with dried rose petals, dried lavender, dried mint, and dried rosemary) as incense. Carnation petals can also be ground down and used to dress a pink candle, burning it to welcome love into your life.

Carnations are associated with protection. Keep dried petals in a pouch hanging in your home to keep away negative energies. To make a protective oil that can be used for anointing yourself, place 3 tsp of dried carnation petals into 7 fl oz (200 ml) of carrier oil such as sunflower or jojoba in an airtight jar. Keep in a cool, dark place and shake daily, leaving it to steep for 3–4 weeks. A carnation tea made by adding 3 tsp of dried carnation petals to 1 cup of

ZODIAC SIGN
Sagittarius

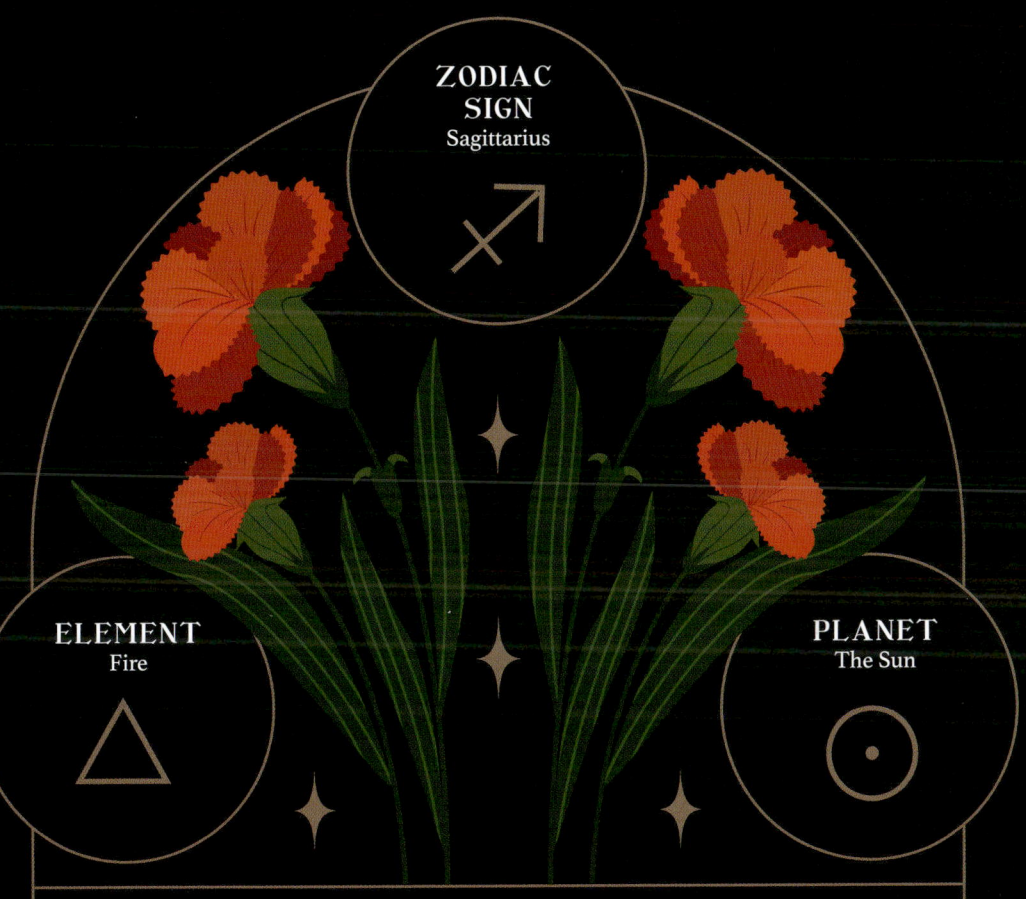

ELEMENT
Fire

PLANET
The Sun

CARNATION
Dianthus caryophyllus

MAGICKAL PROPERTIES
- Attracts love
- Protects
- Helps regain strength
- Removes negative energy and curses
- Increases gratitude

MEDICINAL PROPERTIES
- Treats muscular soreness
- Relieves menstrual cramps
- Treats eczema and rashes
- Soothes nerves
- Relieves stress
- Boosts immune system
- Lifts mood
- Flushes out bodily toxins
- Eases diarrhea
- Helps stomach pains

FOLK NAMES
Gillies, Gilliflower, Jove's Flower, Nelka, Scaffold Flower, Sops-In-Wine

hot water, and steeping for 5–7 minutes, can be drunk or used as a face wash (once cooled) for both personal protection and strength. If you are ill, carnations can be placed in your bedroom to bring healing, and help you regain your strength. Red carnations are an excellent addition to your altar if you are casting any kind of healing spell.

MEDICINAL PROPERTIES

Carnations have inflammatory properties and can treat muscle soreness and menstrual cramps. Use 4 oz (110 g) of petals in a tea or make into a salve (see page 22) with 8 fl oz (230 ml) of carrier oil such as sunflower or jojoba and 1 oz (30 g) of beeswax, and rub onto the affected area. This salve can also treat muscle spasms. Due to its anti-inflammatory properties, a carnation oil (see page 18) made from 2 tsp of carnation petals and 8 fl oz (230 ml) of carrier oil such as sunflower or jojoba can be used to treat eczema and minor skin rashes.

Carnations, brewed as a tea, infusion, or tisane, can help to soothe nerves, combat stress, and lift the mood, as they calm the nervous system. As they are full of antioxidants, they also help to give a boost to your immune system. Carnation tea is cleansing so helps to flush out any toxins in your body, relieve stomach aches, and treat diarrhea.

DISCLAIMER:
Do not to consume any tea or internal preparation made from bought cut flowers unless they are organically grown, as cut flowers may contain traces of poisonous pesticides and artificial fertilizers.

CHRYSANTHEMUM
Chrysanthemum morifolium

FOLKLORE

Native to north-eastern Europe and eastern Asia, chrysanthemums are a symbol of friendship, longevity, and joy. In China, chrysanthemum wine is drunk on the ninth day of the ninth month for good health and peace.

In ancient Greek folklore, chrysanthemums were believed to protect against evil spirits, and were placed on graves. "Chrysanthemum" derives from the Greek words *chrysos*, meaning "gold," and *anthemom*, meaning "flower."

In Japanese folklore, chrysanthemums became a symbol of the Japanese throne when emperor Go-Daigo adopted them as his crest and seal. This flower is even celebrated as a symbol of happiness and joy in the festival Kiku no Sekku (Festival of Happiness). In Christian lore, chrysanthemums were seen as a symbol of death and were associated with All Souls Day, a time of remembrance for the faithfully departed. Chrysanthemums were also a symbol of the hope of the resurrection and life after death, which is why, in the Christian tradition, they were often used at funerals.

MAGICKAL PROPERTIES

Associated with protection, having a vase of chrysanthemums in your home will prevent negative influences from entering your house. Chrysanthemums are also used to remember the dead and are a great addition to your Samhain or ancestor altar. The petals can be burned while communicating with the spirits of your ancestors. The Swedish artist and Witch Hilma af Klint was known for communing with spirits in this way. She incorporated spirit work into her paintings in the form of channeled images and automatic writing. Her most famous creation is called "The Ten Largest."

Chrysanthemums can be made into an oil to bring happiness and joy. In an airtight jar, add 3 tsp of dried yellow chrysanthemum petals and 2 tsp each of chamomile and lemon balm to 14 fl oz (400 ml) of carrier oil such as sunflower or jojoba, and leave to infuse for 3–4 weeks. After this time, drain and discard the petals and herbs before using. Use it to anoint yourself when you need a boost of happiness or to dress candles.

For a simple happiness spell, use the oil to anoint a yellow candle, placing 3 pieces of citrine around it. Let the candle burn out and then carry the citrine with you.

MEDICINAL PROPERTIES

Chrysanthemums are frequently used in traditional Chinese medicine to make tea to promote relaxation. In a cup of hot water, add 2 chrysanthemum flowers and leave to steep for 5–7 minutes. Drink 3 times a day before bed or at times of stress. To help ease headaches, make a tea by brewing the roots of chrysanthemums for 5–10 minutes.

Chrysanthemums can boost immunity due to their high levels of vitamin C, and can be used to treat the symptoms of a cold. To make a tincture, cover 5 tsp of dried chrysanthemums (any colour) in 10 fl oz (300 ml) of vodka, and leave to steep for 4 weeks. Drain and discard the petals before use, and take 15–20 drops, 3 times a day as soon as the symptoms of a cold appears.

DISCLAIMER:
If you are allergic to ragweed or daisies, you may also be allergic to chrysanthemums.

ZODIAC SIGN
Leo
♌

ELEMENT
Fire
△

PLANET
The Sun
☉

CHRYSANTHEMUM
Chrysanthemum morifolium

MAGICKAL PROPERTIES
- Protects
- Wards off negative energy
- Stop arguments
- Cools tempers
- Helps remember the dead and communicate with spirits
- Brings happiness and joy, good health, and longevity

MEDICINAL PROPERTIES
- Promotes relaxation
- Reduces stress
- Promotes heart health
- Eases headaches
- Boosts immunity
- Treats colds and flu
- Aids digestion
- Promotes eye health
- Reduces blood pressure

FOLK NAMES Button and Spray, Chrysanthemum, Daisy, Mums, Pompon

ZODIAC SIGN
Leo

ELEMENT
Fire

PLANET
The Sun

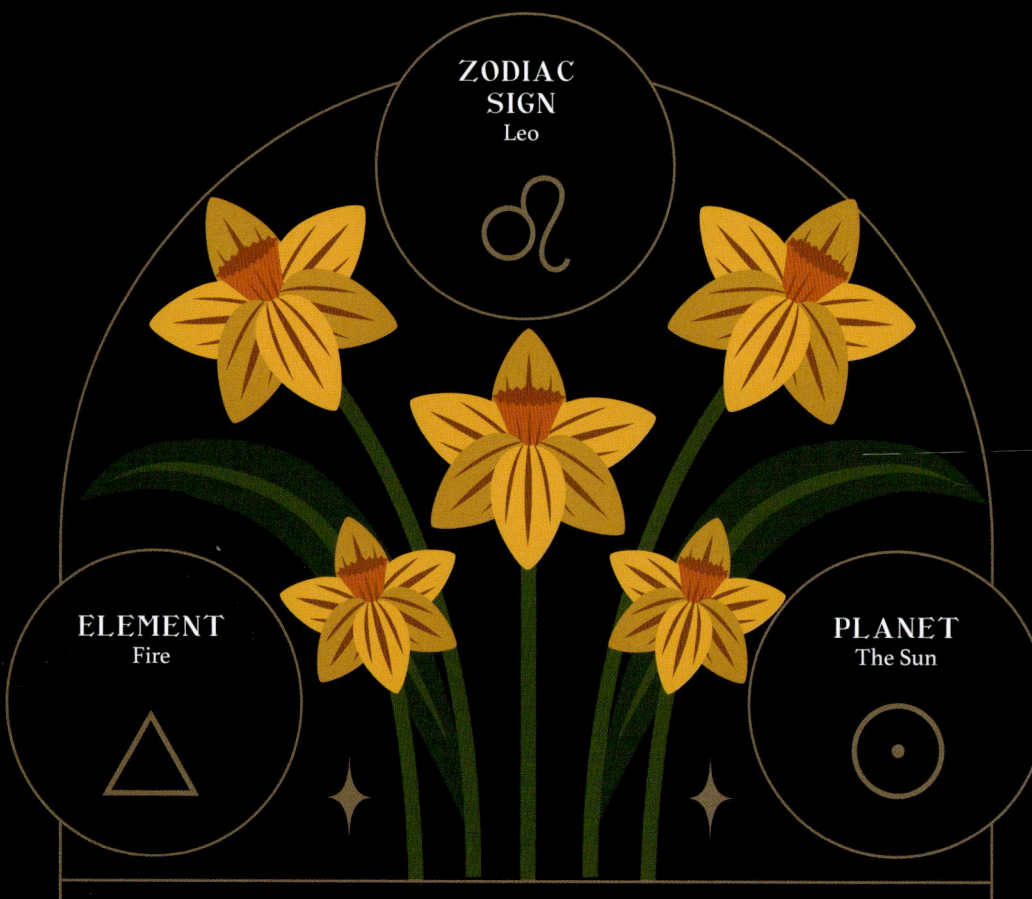

DAFFODIL
Narcissus

MAGICKAL PROPERTIES
- Promotes love and self love
- Symbolizes birth and hope
- Brings joy, good luck, prosperity, and peace
- Boosts resilience and brings abundance
- Protects

FOLK NAMES
Bell Rose, Daffadowndilly, Lent Lily, Easter Lily

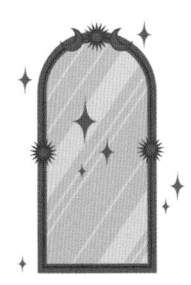

DAFFODIL
Narcissus

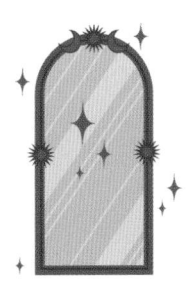

FOLKLORE

Originally from Europe and northern Africa, daffodils are steeped in mythology. They symbolize new birth and hope, as they're the first flowers to bloom in springtime. In Victorian England, daffodils signified unrequited love, as well as respect and prosperity.

In ancient Greek folklore, daffodils are the flower of the dead, and are associated with the god Hades. Another Greek myth is connected to the god Narcissus, who was granted immortal good looks for as long as he didn't see his own reflection. A wood nymph called Echo fell in love with Narcissus, but he was only interested in himself, and the nymph eventually pined away from unrequited love. The goddess Nemesis wanted revenge for what Narcissus had done to the nymph, so she showed him his own refection in a lake. He died, and daffodils bloomed where his body fell. Despite this mythology, in the Middle East, daffodils are considered an aphrodisiac and symbolize a faithful lover.

In Christianity, daffodils were said to have appeared to comfort Jesus in the Garden of Gethsemane after Judas betrayed him. In Scandinavian countries, daffodils are also connected to Christian lore and are called Easter lily because they bloom at Easter time.

MAGICKAL PROPERTIES

Daffodils are highly toxic and should not be consumed. Even the stalk sap can cause a rash when in contact with the skin, so wear gloves when handling this flower. They have no medicinal uses.

Daffodils are a great addition to your Ostara altar to mark the beginning of spring. Plant daffodil bulbs in your yard in fall so they bloom in time for spring.

Daffodils are associated with good luck, resilience, abundance, and regeneration. To welcome abundance into your home, place daffodils in a vase in your home. You can also plant daffodil bulbs in your yard near your front door to draw in more abundance and to protect your home from negative energies.

DAISY
Bellis perennis

FOLKLORE

Often considered a weed, daisies originate from Europe and temperate regions in Asia, but can now be found on every continent except Antarctica.

In Christian lore, the Virgin Mary was picking daisies for Jesus when she pricked her finger, and stained the flowers with her blood, turning the tips of the flower pink. It was also believed that daisies were given by God to bring comfort to those parents whose children had died. This came from a Celtic story about a woman named Malvina who was grieving the death of her stillborn son, but was consoled after hearing that dead children were reincarnated as daisies.

In ancient Rome, daisies were associated with Vertumnus, god of seasons and gardens. He fell in love with a nymph called Belides, but to avoid his unwanted attention, she turned herself into a daisy.

MAGICKAL PROPERTIES

Daises are associated with love, friendship, and divination. As a child you may have pulled the petals from a daisy, repeating the words "she/he loves me, she/he loves me not" to find out if your love interest liked you. This is a simple love spell that can be used by adults too. The petals can be pulled off in the same way for yes/no answers. To reignite and strengthen love in a romantic or platonic relationship, fill a pouch with daisies and either sleep with them under your pillow or carry them with you.

Daisies are associated with faerie magick and daisy chains make great offerings to the Fae at Beltane and the summer solstice. At these times of year, daisies can also be used to decorate your home to welcome in good luck, happiness, joy, and abundance. The 17th-century Scottish Witch Isobel Gowdie was known for communing with the Fae at this time of year. She claimed, not under duress, at her trial that she had been entertained by the queen of the faeries.

ZODIAC SIGN
Taurus

ELEMENT
Earth

PLANETS
The Sun and Venus

DAISY
Bellis perennis

MAGICKAL PROPERTIES
- Strengthens love and friendship
- Increases good luck
- Brings happiness, joy, and abundance

MEDICINAL PROPERTIES
- Treats coughs and colds
- Relieves aches and pains
- Treats cuts, wounds, and bruises
- Aids digestion
- Improves circulation

FOLK NAMES
Bairnwort, Banewort, Banwood, Billy Button, Bruisewort, Child's Flower, Day's Eye, Ewe-Gowan, Field Daisy, Flower Of Spring, Gowan, Herb Margaret, Little Star, Llygad y Dydd, Maudlinwort, Measure Of Love, Moon Daisy, Open Eye, Silver Pennies

MEDICINAL PROPERTIES

Daisies can treat coughs and colds. As an expectorant (which helps loosen mucus so you can cough it up effectively and clear your throat and lungs), an infusion can be made with a large handful of daisies and drunk 3 times a day for as long at the symptoms persist (see page 14). Daisy syrup is also great for soothing coughs and sore throats. To make a daisy syrup, boil 3.5 oz (100 g) of daisy leaves, flowers, and stalks in enough water to cover them in a pan for 20 minutes. Strain and discard the daisies and add an equal amount of honey to the amount of water left in the pan. Boil it until the mixture thickens. Take 1 tbsp 3 times a day until the cough has gone.

Daisies have anti-inflammatory and antibacterial properties. For aches and pains, a daisy salve can be made from 8 fl oz (235 ml) of daisy infused oil and 1 oz (30 g) of beeswax, and rubbed onto painful areas of the body. For cuts, bites, wounds, and bruises, use a daisy poultice (see page 28). Place a large handful of daisy flowers in a muslin bag. Soak the bag in hot water for 5 minutes and apply the paste to the affected area for 15 minutes.

DANDELION
Taraxacum officinale

FOLKLORE

Dandelions are native to Eurasia and their name is derived from the French *dent de lion*, meaning "lion's tooth" due to its jagged petals.

In English folklore, dandelions were known as piss-a-bed because it was believed they could make you wet the bed, as the leaf is a powerful diuretic. In the Middle Ages, it was believed that if you held a dandelion under your chin and your skin appeared yellow, it meant you would get rich in the future. If you also blew on a dandelion clock and made a wish, the seeds would carry your wish, and if they were kept in your house, dandelions would protect animals and humans from Witchcraft.

MAGICKAL PROPERTIES

Dandelion are used in love divination. If you think of your love interest and blow on a dandelion clock, it will show you how loved you are. If you blow all the seeds away completely, your love interest is infatuated with you. If some seeds remain, they have some reservations or doubts. Divination, particularly love divination, was practiced by many Witches in time gone by, such as Ursula Southeil, better known as Mother Shipton. She lived in Yorkshire, and many people would visit her from near and far because of her divinatory gifts.

Dandelions increase psychic abilities. Take 4 clean dandelion roots and hang them in a cool, dry room until they are fully dry, then roast them at 350°F (180° C) for 30 minutes until they are brown (but not burned). Grind them down and use them to make an infusion by steeping them in hot (but not boiling) water for 20 minutes. This infusion also helps to increase bravery and courage, and placed near your bed at night, will help to summon spirits.

MEDICINAL PROPERTIES

Dandelions have anti-inflammatory properties and can help relieve muscular pain and arthritis. Place 5 clean dandelion roots in a jar, cover with vodka, and leave to infuse for 1 month, shaking daily. Drain away the plant matter and take 15 drops of the tincture in a little water, 3 times a day. It can also be used for treating indigestion.

Dandelion tea can help to lower blood pressure, aid in blood sugar regulation, reduce high cholesterol, and even promote liver health. To make a tea, steep the flowers and leaves in hot water for 15 minutes. Drink 3 times a day.

ZODIAC SIGN
Sagittarius

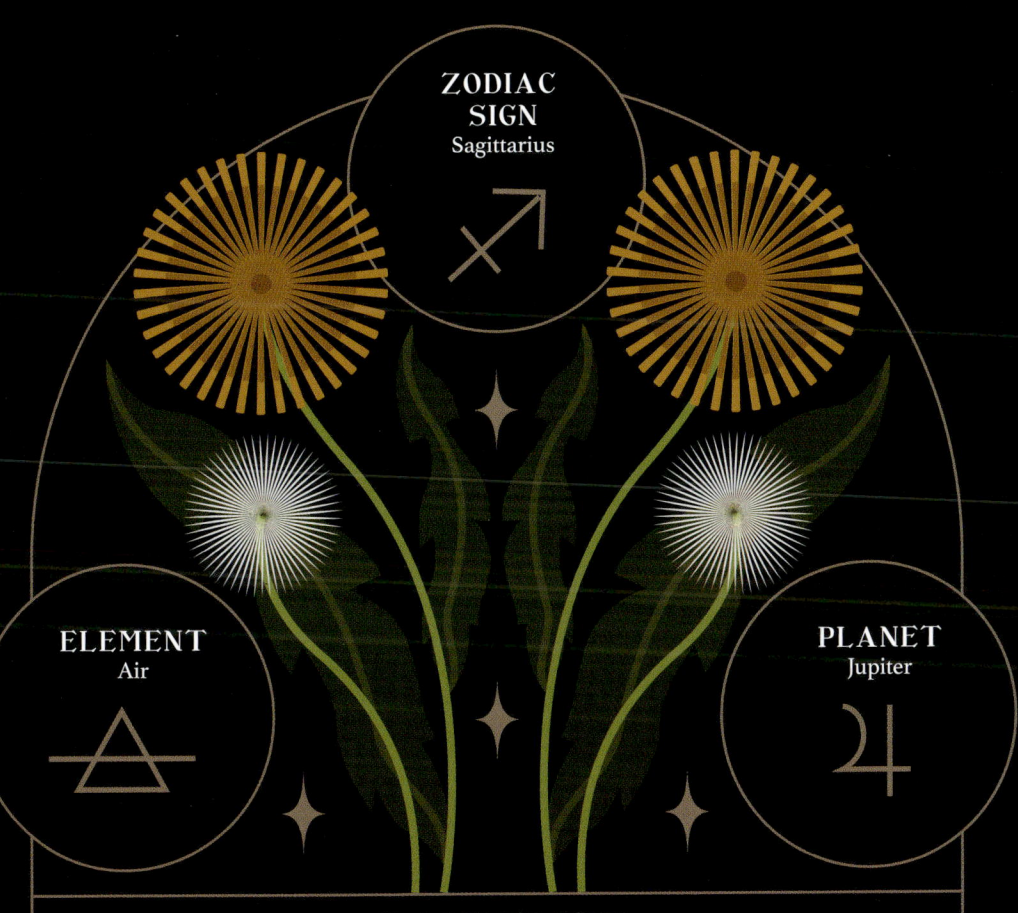

ELEMENT
Air

PLANET
Jupiter

DANDELION
Taraxacum officinale

MAGICKAL PROPERTIES
- Increases psychic abilities, bravery, and courage
- Summons spirits
- Encourages growth, hope, transformation, and new beginnings

MEDICINAL PROPERTIES
- Treats muscular pain
- Eases arthritis
- Lowers blood pressure
- Regulates blood sugar
- Reduces cholesterol
- Promotes liver health

FOLK NAMES Blowball, Cankerwort, Lion's Tooth, Piss-a-bed, Priest's Crown, Puffball, Swine's Snout, White Endive, Wild Endive

ZODIAC SIGN
Cancer

ELEMENT
Water

PLANETS
Venus and the Moon

JASMINE
Jasminum grandiflorum

MAGICKAL PROPERTIES
- Used for love and purity
- Boosts prophetic dreaming, psychic abilities, and intuition
- Brings peace and balance

MEDICINAL PROPERTIES
- Sedates
- Relieves stress
- Induces relaxation
- Improves sleep
- Reduces scarring
- Boosts brain function
- Lifts the mood
- Eases stomach pain
- Treats diarrhea

FOLK NAMES Flower of Kings, Flower of Queens, Kessamin, Moonlight on the Grove, Poet's Jasmine, Queen of the Night

JASMINE
Jasminum grandiflorum

FOLKLORE

Known as the Queen of Flowers, jasmine is thought to be native to Asia and the Middle East. In Buddhism, it is associated with devotion and purity. In 1819, cave wall paintings were discovered in India that depicted princesses wearing tiaras made from jasmine. In Hinduism, jasmine is a symbol of love and is used in bridal wedding garlands. Like Cupid, Manmatha, the Hindu god of love would also shoot arrows made of jasmine to make people fall in love.

In Arab folklore, there was a tale of a beautiful nomad called Jasmine who roamed the desert sands. A north African prince wanted to see if this woman was real, so he went to the desert looking for her, eventually finding her walking through the dunes. He instantly fell in love with her and asked her to marry him. She accepted his proposal and agreed to live with him in his palace, but after a while, she began to miss the desert. One night, she escaped and went back to the place where she felt she belonged. The sun was so glad that she had returned home that it decided to immortalize her into the flower we know today as jasmine.

MAGICKAL PROPERTIES

Jasmine is associated with love and affection. Use dried jasmine flowers as potpourri to attract love into your home. Jasmine is considered one of the best oils for dressing candles for this purpose. Place 4 tsp of dried jasmine in 5 fl oz (150 ml) of oil and leave to steep for 4 weeks before draining out the flowers. Dress a pink candle in the oil and burn it to attract love.

Associated with money, jasmine can be carried or burned to attract wealth. Use dried jasmine flowers to dress and then burn a green candle that is inscribed with the rune Fehu to attract money, abundance, and prosperity.

Jasmine induces prophetic dreaming. Burn jasmine flowers in your bedroom as incense before you go to sleep, or place 3–4 drops of jasmine essential oil on your pillow to enhance your psychic abilities and intuition.

MEDICINAL PROPERTIES

Jasmine is used as a sedative and can help to relax nervous tension and induce sleep. Carry a bottle of jasmine essential oil in your pocket and smell its fragrance when you are feeling stressed to calm your nerves. Take a hot bath with 4–5 drops of jasmine essential oil to induce relaxation and improve sleep. The jasmine in the water can also help to reduce the appearance of scarring and is a potent anti-inflammatory.

As jasmine naturally contains caffeine, a jasmine infusion can help improve cognitive function. Steep 2 tsp of dried jasmine flowers and 2 tsp of rosemary in a cup of hot water for 15 minutes, and drink anytime you need a brain boost. An infusion of jasmine can help to release serotonin and dopamine, which can enhance your mood. It will also aid digestion, relieving abdominal pain and symptoms of irritable bowel syndrome.

PRIMROSE
Primula vulgaris

FOLKLORE

Primroses are native to western and southern Europe. In Irish folklore, primroses were used to connect with the Fae. It was believed that large patches of primroses were a sign there is an entrance to the faerie realm nearby, and primroses were known as "faerie cups." Those who protected these flowers were said to receive a blessing from the Fae, but those who picked them would have bad luck placed upon them.

In England during the 1600s, primroses were associated with a life cut short. If a woman died young and unmarried, a garland of primroses and other spring flowers were placed on her grave to represent that she was cut down in the springtime of her life. It was believed that after death she would turn into primroses. Primroses were believed to be Shakespeare's favorite flower, and feature in many of his plays.

MAGICKAL PROPERTIES

Primroses can be used to connect with the Fae. According to Irish folklore, hanging primroses by your front door will invite in faeries and ask for their blessings. If primroses are scattered outside your door, however, it will stop the Fae from crossing the threshold. Hanging primroses by the doors of your home can protect it from negative and unwanted energies and people. The Irish Witch Biddy Early was famous for her work with the Fae and declared that all her herbal and healing knowledge came from the Fae and the time that she spent with them.

Primroses can be used for rejuvenation. Collect them early in the morning at Ostara so they are covered with morning dew, and use them to make a tea or infusion to restore youthful vigor (see pages 12–14). To rejuvenate the skin, soak primroses in warm water for 15 minutes and then use the water as a face wash.

MEDICINAL PROPERTIES

Due to its anti-inflammatory properties, primroses soothe rashes and eczema. Take a handful of primrose flowers and place them in warm water, leaving them to infuse in the sun for 45 minutes. Once ready, drain out the flowers and use the infusion to cleanse the affected area twice a day. A salve can also be made from 4 tsp of primrose flowers infused in 8.5 fl oz (250 ml) of oil and 1 oz (30 g) of beeswax for more persistent skin conditions (see page 22).

As an expectorant, primroses can be used to treat coughs, colds, and respiratory issues. A primrose syrup stirred into hot water and drunk 3 times a day can relieve these conditions. To make a syrup, use 5 tbsp of primrose flowers, 7.5 oz (215 g) honey, 8.5 fl oz (250 ml) water and 3 fl oz (90 ml) of brandy. Dissolve the honey into the water by boiling it in a pan. Once dissolved, take the pan off the heat and add the other ingredients. After 24 hours, drain and discard the flowers and it's ready to use.

ZODIAC SIGN
Taurus

ELEMENT
Earth

PLANET
Venus

PRIMROSE
Primula vulgaris

MAGICKAL PROPERTIES
- Protects
- Removes negative energy
- Rejuvenates
- Restores youthful vigor
- Promotes good luck
- Attracts prosperity
- Induces prophetic dreams

MEDICINAL PROPERTIES
- Treats arthritis and rheumatism
- Soothes eczema and rashes
- Treats coughs and colds
- Improves respiratory problems
- Relives symptoms of menopause
- Eases menstrual pain
- Regulates hormones
- Improves acne

FOLK NAMES Bears Ears, Buckie Faalie, Faery Cup, Faulie Pumrock, Goslings, Maisie Spink, May Floore, Meysie Spink

POPPY
Papaver

FOLKLORE

There are many varieties of poppies, but the red poppy is native to much of Europe and Asia and is associated with sleep and death. The ancient Egyptians, Romans, and Greeks used poppies as a folk remedy for insomnia and to treat pain. These cultures also gave poppies as offerings to the dead. In ancient Mesopotamia, records show they used the opium extracted from the poppy for the euphoric effect it induced. In ancient Greece, Hypnos the god of sleep often carried a poppy with him. In another Greek myth, the goddess Demeter fell in love with a man called Mekon, turning him into a poppy when he died.

Red poppies are a symbol of remembrance and were believed to grow in places where men died in battle. This is described in the 1915 poem "In Flanders Fields" by John McCrae who described how poppies grew in the trenches during World War I.

MAGICKAL PROPERTIES

Poppies are associated with sleep and dreams. Place 3 tbsp of poppy seeds into a pouch with lavender and hops and put it under your pillow for a restful night's sleep. To make dreams more vivid, use poppy seeds and mugwort to dress a purple candle and burn before you go to sleep.

With its association with death, poppies can be used as offerings to remember loved ones that have passed away. Place a jar of poppy seeds on your altar at Samhain to honor your ancestors, especially those who were part of military.

Associated with relaxation, make an incense made from 1 tsp each of poppy seeds, dried chamomile, dried lavender, dried valerian, and dried lemon balm to bring a sense of calm. Burn 1 tsp of the incense on a charcoal disc whenever you're struggling to relax.

ZODIAC SIGN
Gemini

ELEMENT
Water

PLANET
The Moon

POPPY
Papaver

MAGICKAL PROPERTIES
- Aids sleep and dreams
- Helps remember loved ones
- Relaxes
- Increases love, prosperity, and money

MEDICINAL PROPERTIES
- Treats insomnia
- Encourages relaxation
- Regulates blood pressure
- Reduces cholesterol
- Improves brain health
- Treats diarrhea
- Aids digestion
- Strengthens bones

FOLK NAMES Cop Rose, Cup Rose, Daughter of the Fields, Thunderflower, Tintenblume

MEDICINAL PROPERTIES

Poppies can help to fight insomnia. Steep a cup of tea with 1 tsp each of poppy seeds, lavender, and passionflower for 5–7 minutes, and enjoy with a little honey before bed. A tincture can also be made from 3 tsp each of the above ingredients and 8.5 fl oz (250 ml) of vodka. Leave to infuse for 5 weeks before draining and discarding the plant matter. Take 15–20 drops under the tongue or in water 3 times a day.

Poppy seeds are known to help regulate blood pressure. Make a tea by combining 1 tsp each of poppy seeds, dried thyme, dried basil, cinnamon, and a slice of fresh ginger, and brewing for 20 minutes. Drink 2–3 times a day. Due to the abundance of dietary fibre in poppy seeds, this infusion can also help to improve blood circulation and stabilizes the amount of good cholesterol in the body.

ROSE
Rosa

FOLKLORE

Most species of roses are native to Asia, however, some originated from Africa and Europe. According to Persian folklore, the tears of the prophet Muhammad created the rose when his daughter, Fatima, fell ill.

In ancient Greek mythology, roses were associated with Aphrodite. When her lover Adonis was hurt while hunting, she rushed to his side and accidentally scratched herself on a rose thorn, turning the white roses to red with her blood.

In ancient Rome, the goddess Flora found the body of a nymph when she was walking through the woods, and decided to turn her into a flower. She called on the god Apollo to shine sun on the nymph's body, asked Bacchus to give the flower nectar, and asked Vertumnus to provide fragrance, thus creating the rose.

In Christian lore, roses grew without thorns until Adam and Eve were banished from the Garden of Eden. The roses then had thorns due to the wickedness of Eve.

MAGICKAL PROPERTIES

Roses are associated with love, romance and beauty. To attract love, prepare a hot bath and add red rose petals for love and pink rose petals for friendship along with 5 drops of rose essential oil. Take this bath whenever you want to bring more love into your relationships.

To sweeten a romantic relationship, make a spell jar with red rose petals, rose quartz, honey, and your name and the name of your love written on a piece of paper, sealing the lid with red candle wax. Carry it with you when you are with the person for whom the jar was made for.

To make a crystal-infused water for beauty, place 4 tsp of dried red rose petals, a piece of rose quartz, clear quartz, and amethyst in a jug of water and leave to infuse for 24 hours. Drain and discard the rose petals and crystals before drinking throughout the day. This water can also be used to encourage emotional healing if you also add 4 tsp each of lemon balm and chamomile.

MEDICINAL PROPERTIES

Roses have antibacterial and anti-inflammatory properties. To make rose water for wounds and easing muscular pains, simmer 10 tsp of rose petals with enough water to cover them in a pan for 30 minutes before straining out the petals. You can use it to clean wounds, to stop infection, and rub onto painful parts of the body. Keep refrigerated for up to 8 days. Alternatively, you can make a rose salve for the same purpose, using, use 10 oz (280 g) of rose petals and 1 oz (30 g) of beeswax (see page 22).

Roses are a nervine and can help uplift the mood and alleviate depression. Make a tea from 1 tsp each of rose petals, lemon balm, hawthorn leaves, and lavender in a cup of hot (but not boiling) water, and steep for 15 minutes, drinking 3 times a day.

ZODIAC SIGN
Taurus

ELEMENT
Water

PLANET
Venus

ROSE
Rosa

MAGICKAL PROPERTIES
- Increases love, romance, beauty, and self love
- Sweetens relationships
- Increases lust
- Boosts intuition and confidence
- Aids dream work

MEDICINAL PROPERTIES
- Eases muscular pains
- Cleans wounds
- Lifts the mood
- Eases depression

FOLK NAMES Queen of Flowers

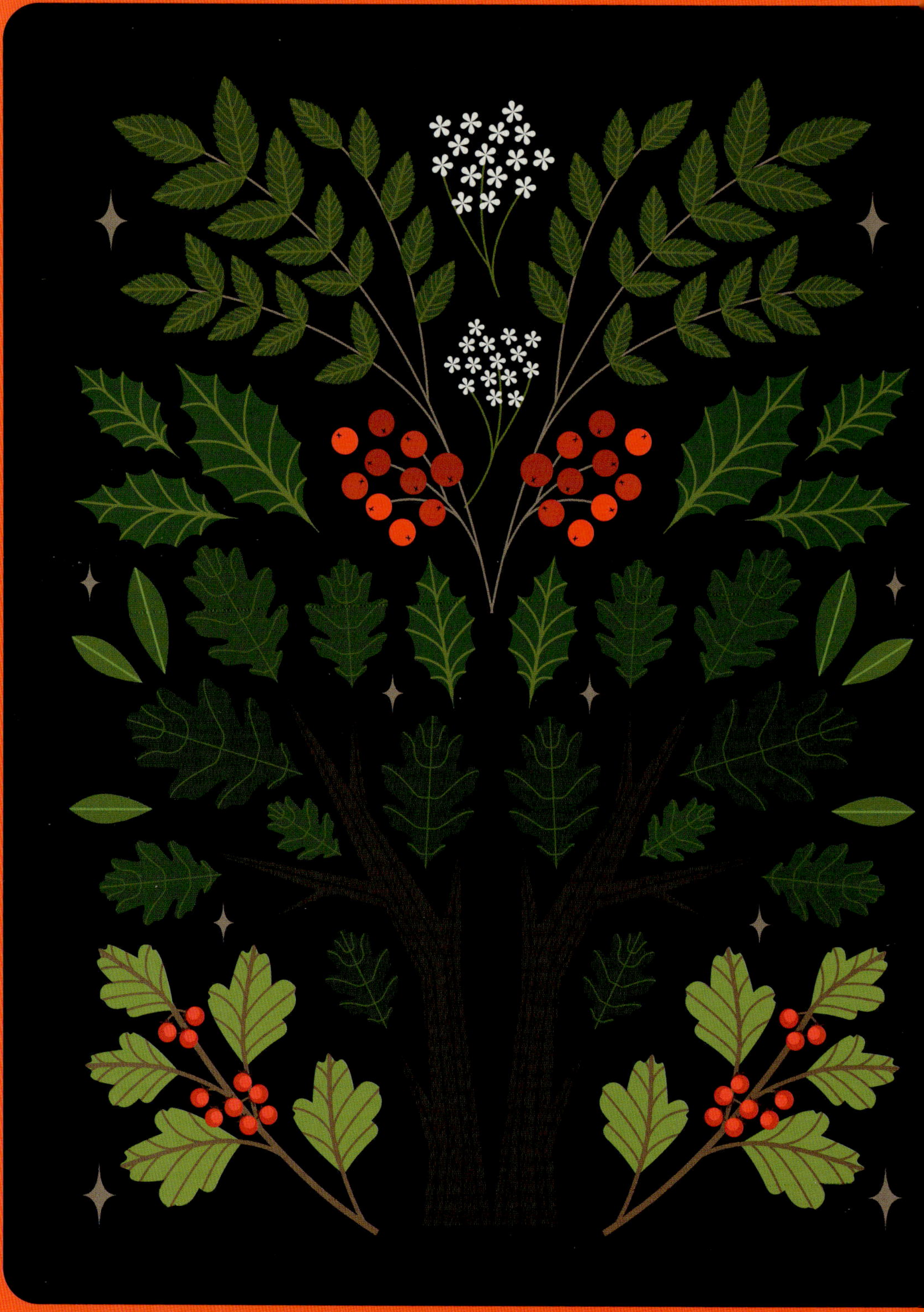

3
TREES

Trees have played a large role in Witchcraft and medicinal healing practices for thousands of years, and there is much folklore associated with the trees we find around us. Many cultures and civilizations have their different myths and stories about the trees that grew around them. For example, the Celts believed that the oak tree ruled the lighter half of the year and the holly tree ruled the darker half of the year. Instead of zodiac signs, the Celts used the Celtic tree calendar where each month was aligned to a different tree, which represented the changing of the year.

    This chapter will focus upon more of the rich folklore and mythology associated with many well-known and commonly found trees. It will also include the range of their magickal properties and how you can use them in in your own spells and rituals as well as how to incorporate them into your healing practices like the cunning folk of ages past.

BIRCH
Betula pendula

FOLKLORE

Birch trees are native to many countries across the Northern Hemisphere.

In Celtic folklore, birch trees represent new beginnings, purification, and renewal. At Samhain (the Witch's new year) birch twigs were burned on fires to ward off evil, and besoms were made from the twigs in order to purify the home. Birch twigs were also hung over doorways to protect against negative energies.

At Beltane, the Celts would make maypoles from birch wood for their fertility dances, and they believed that the trees contained the souls of their ancestors. These trees were sacred to the goddess Brigid in Irish mythology, as it was thought that she was born under a birch. In Scotland, birch trees were believed to protect against lightning strikes as they would absorb the lightning energy, so they were often planted near homes. In England, birch trees were often used for the protection of land and to mark property lines.

MAGICKAL PROPERTIES

Birch trees are considered protective. To ward off negative energy, tie a small bundle of birch twigs together with a piece of red ribbon or red string and hang them in the window of your home.

Long associated with purification, dry birch twigs can be tied together in a bundle and burned. Fan the smoke into every corner of your space or room to remove negative or unwanted energies.

For new beginnings magick, take a piece of birch tree bark at the New Moon and write on it about the kind of new start you are looking for. Afterward, burn the bark to release the energy of your spell.

ZODIAC SIGNS
Gemini and Sagittarius

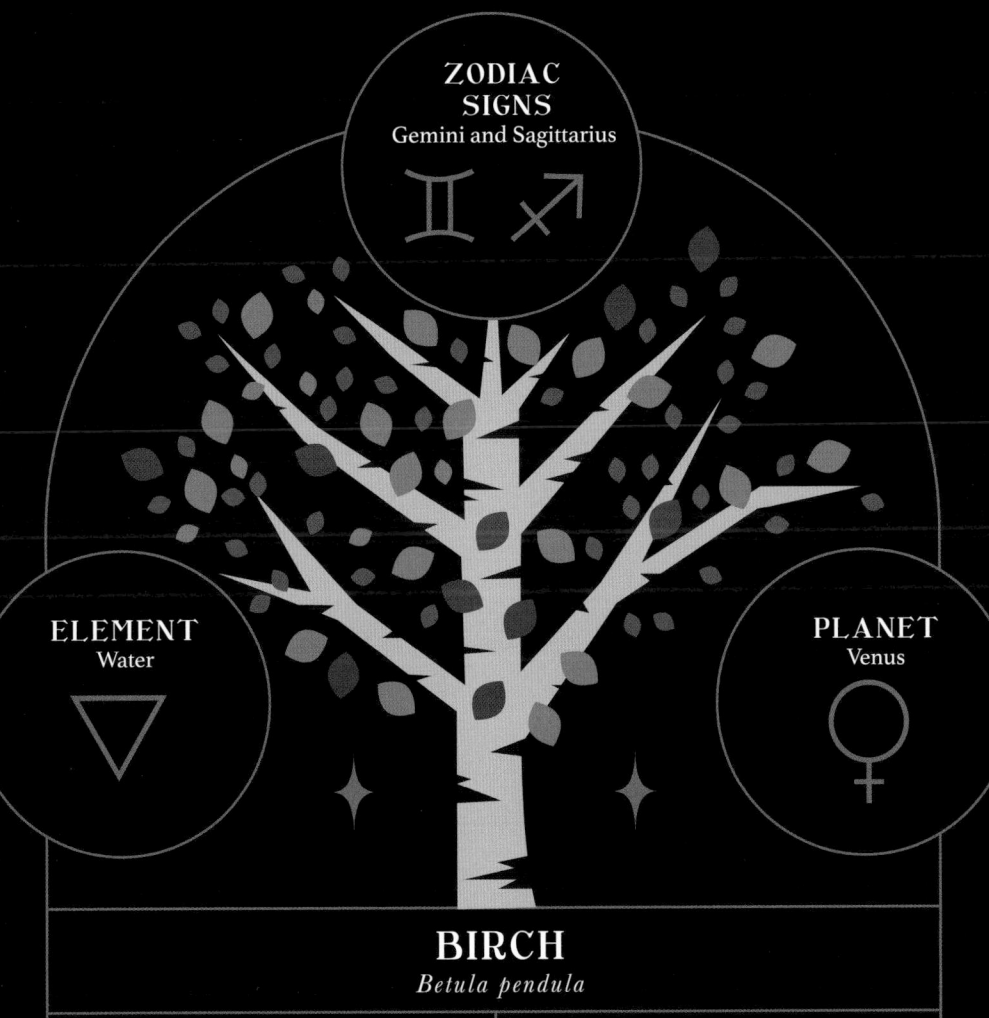

ELEMENT
Water

PLANET
Venus

BIRCH
Betula pendula

MAGICKAL PROPERTIES
- Protects
- Wards off negative energy
- Purifies
- Brings new beginnings
- Banishes evil
- Renews

MEDICINAL PROPERTIES
- Relieves urinary tract infections
- Relieves pain
- Eases headaches
- Treats sprains
- Clears sinuses

FOLK NAMES Beithe, Genii of the Forest, Lady of the Woods

MEDICINAL PROPERTIES

Birch leaves have antiseptic and antibacterial properties. To prevent wound infection, make a poultice from birch leaves and twigs. Grind down equal amounts of the leaves and twigs with a mortar and pestle and add them to a muslin bag. Soak in hot water for 15 minutes. After this time, place the bag on the wound for 20 minutes.

As a diuretic, 4 tsp of dried, ground birch leaves can be made into a tea using a tea ball infuser. Steep in hot water for 10 minutes to treat water retention and high blood pressure. This tea can also bring relief if you're suffering from cystitis or a urinary tract infection.

The birch tree has anti-inflammatory and analgesic properties. A tincture can be made by adding 2 tsp each of dried ground birch leaves and twigs to 10 fl oz (300 ml) vodka or brandy, and leaving for 4–5 weeks to infuse. After this time, drain an discard the tree matter and keep in a jar, taking 15 drops under the tongue, 3 times a day. This tincture can help to relive inflammation and can be taken to reduce pain.

ELDER
Sambucus nigra

FOLKLORE

Elder trees are native to the UK, Europe, south west Asia and north Africa.

In Celtic folklore, the elder represents change, transformation, and spiritual renewal. Witches favored the wood to make their wands with because of its protective qualities. They were also planted near homes to protect them from negativity, lightning, and Witchcraft.

In Scandinavian folklore, before an elder tree is cut, used in spells, or touched, a person must first gain the permission of Mother Elder, who inhabited the tree.

In Christian lore, Christ was crucified on a cross made from elder wood, and Judas hung himself from an elder tree, so it became associated with sorrow and death. In Christian England, burning elder wood was believed to raise the Devil, and any food that was cooked on a fire made from elder wood would be unfit for consumption.

MAGICKAL PROPERTIES

The elder is protective and can remove curses. Place dried elder leaves and berries, black salt, and agrimony into a pouch and carry it with you until the curse is eliminated. You can also use dried elder leaves, agrimony, and black salt to dress a black candle inscribed with the rune Elhaz. Once the candle has burned out, the curse is removed. One Witch who famously removed curses in 17th-century France was Catherine Monvoisin, also known as La Voisin.

To protect your home, hang some elder twigs near the doors of your home. A protective wash can also be made from elder to wash hard surfaces in your home. To make, place 4 handfuls of elder leaves and berries in a bucket of hot water and leave to infuse for 30 minutes. Then drain and discard the tree matter and use the water to clean your floors, walls, and windows.

The berries from the elder tree can aid astral travel. Create a tea made from a handful of cooked, dried elderberries in a cup of hot water for 20 minutes and drink before bed.

ZODIAC SIGN
Sagittarius

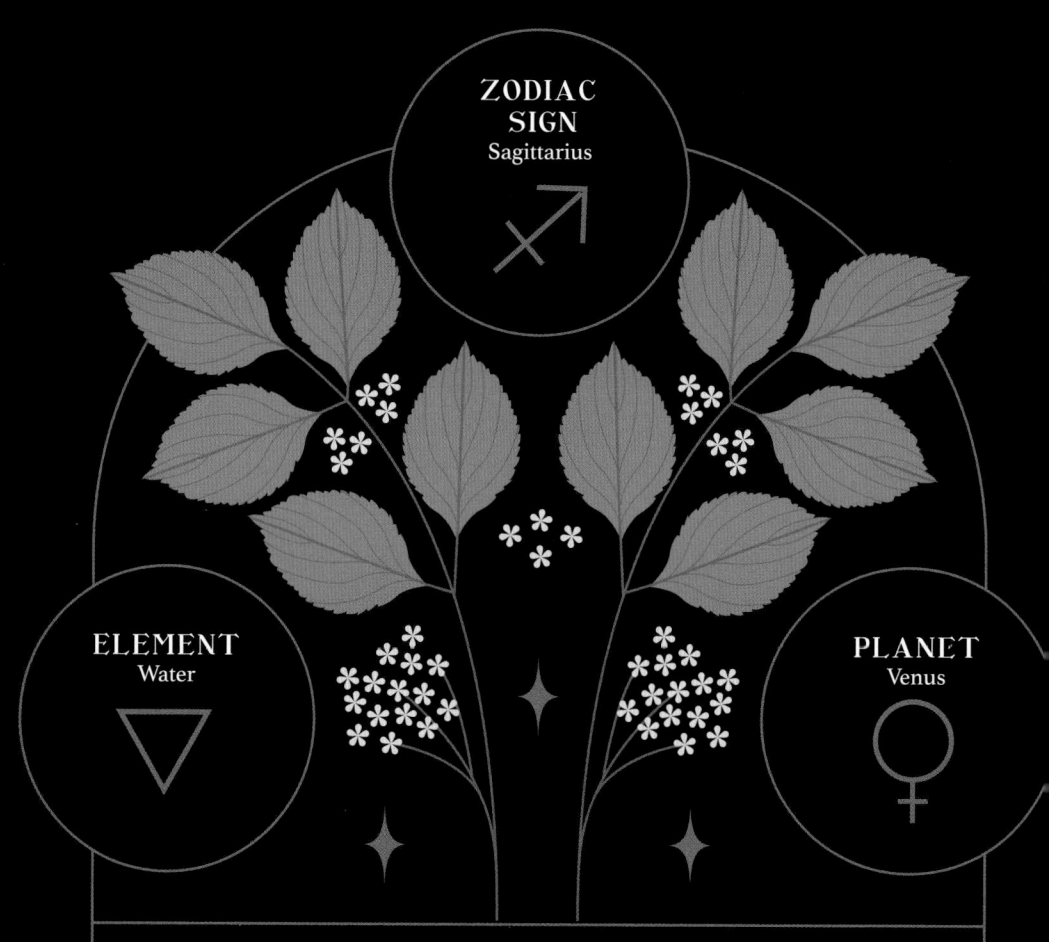

ELEMENT
Water

PLANET
Venus

ELDER
Sambucus nigra

MAGICKAL PROPERTIES
- Protects from harm and evil spirits
- Breaks spells
- Boosts strength, creativity, and health
- Brings prosperity, abundance, and stability

MEDICINAL PROPERTIES
- Treats colds and flu
- Relieves sinus problems
- Reduces fevers
- Aids digestion
- Treats arthritis
- Boosts immune system
- Treats hayfever

FOLK NAMES
Battree, Boure Tree, Hylder, Old Gal, Pipe Tree, Rob Elder, Sweet Elder, Tree of Doom

MEDICINAL PROPERTIES

Elder wood has anti-inflammatory properties. To relieve rheumatism and pain, a folk remedy was to carry the elder tree's green wood in your pocket.

With antiviral and antibacterial properties, elder can treat respiratory infections. To make elder tea, place 2 tbsp of dried elder berries in a mason jar or tea pot and fill completely with boiling water. Leave to steep in the water overnight until the berries are soft and cooked through. Enjoy the next day either hot or cold, adding honey to taste. A syrup can also be made for this purpose by simmering 4 tbsp each of elder berries and leaves for 20 minutes. Next, drain and discard the tree matter, then add 13.5 fl oz (400 ml) each of water and honey to the existing water, and the juice of one lemon. Simmer on a low heat until the liquid has thickened to a syrup. Take 1 tbsp, 3 times a day.

DISCLAIMER:
Do not consume raw elder berries.

HAWTHORN
Crataegus monogyna

FOLKLORE

Hawthorn is native to Europe, Asia, north Africa and North America.

For the Celts, hawthorn was believed to ward off the undead. It was also thought that inhaling the fragrance of the blossoms would enable you to communicate with spirits and connect with the Underworld.

In ancient Greek folklore, hawthorn was associated with marriage, and sprays of the tree would be held over a newly married couple for protection, and to ensure a happy marriage.

In Anglo-Saxon times, hawthorn trees were known as hagedorn trees, meaning "hedge thorn," because farmers would use the trees to mark the boundaries of their land. They were also planted to protect animals and crops from Witchcraft.

MAGICKAL PROPERTIES

Hawthorn can help to heal a broken heart and ease grief. Make a cup of tea with a handful of dried hawthorn berries and add 1 tsp of yarrow, steeping them in hot water for 20 minutes so that the water becomes deeply colored. Drink every day for as long as your heartache or grief remains.

Associated with the spring, hawthorn brings the birth of new beginnings and can help to open the heart to new possibilities. Make an oil from 5 tbsp of hawthorn flowers and 12 fl oz (350 ml) of oil, leaving to infuse for 4 weeks. After this time, carve the symbol for the heart chakra into the wax of a pink candle, then cover it in the oil, before rolling the candle in ground, dried hawthorn berries. As the candle burns, say: "My heart is open to new starts and possibilities." Leave the candle to burn out completely.

DISCLAIMER:
Avoid hawthorn if you are pregnant, breastfeeding or on blood medication.

ZODIAC SIGN
Gemini
♊

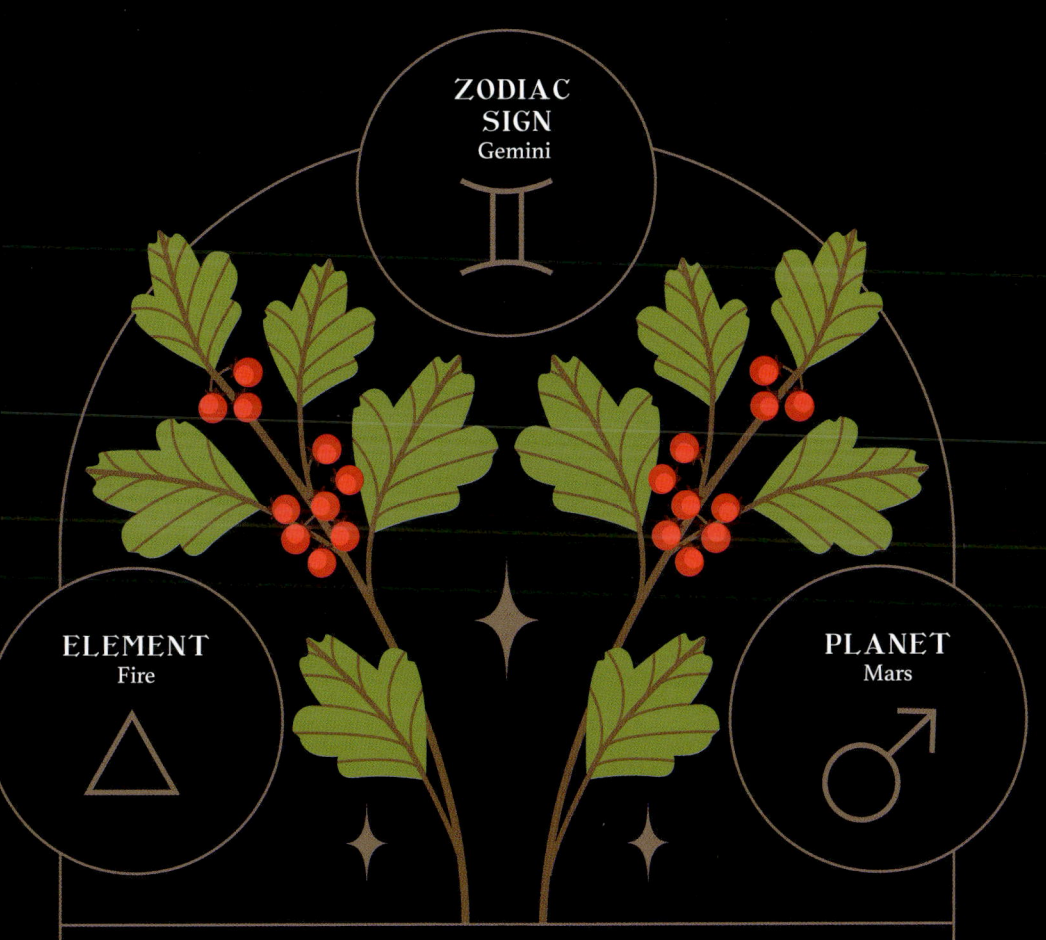

ELEMENT
Fire
△

PLANET
Mars
♂

HAWTHORN
Crataegus monogyna

MAGICKAL PROPERTIES
- Heals broken hearts and grief
- Helps overcome mental exhaustion
- Gives emotional protection
- Welcomes new beginnings
- Opens the heart to new possibilities
- Increases fertility
- Wards off evil spirits

MEDICINAL PROPERTIES
- Supports heart health
- Treats angina
- Regulates heartbeat
- Maintains liver health
- Controls blood pressure
- Reduces cholesterol
- Boosts immune system

FOLK NAMES May Tree, One-Seed Hawthorn, Quickthorn, Thornapple, Whitethorn

MEDICINAL PROPERTIES

Hawthorn is known to improve cardiovascular health. It can help treat angina and an irregular heartbeat, lower high blood pressure, and reduce cholesterol. It is full of antioxidants, which reduce oxidative stress to improve circulation when consumed every day. Crush around 35 oz (1 kg) of hawthorn berries in a pan, then add 35 fl oz (1 liter) of water and simmer for 15–20 minutes. Strain the juice through a cheesecloth and add 16 oz (450 g) of honey, reducing the mixture on a low heat until it becomes a syrup. Take 1 tsp, 3 times a day. This syrup can also be used to treat digestive issues and constipation.

Hawthorn has anti-inflammatory properties too. To make a tea, fill a tea ball infuser with dried hawthorn berries and leave to steep in hot water for 25 minutes. Drink this tea twice a day to help with pain associated with inflammation. This can also help to maintain good liver health.

HOLLY
Ilex aquifolium

FOLKLORE

In Christian lore, the spiky leaves of the holly tree were connected to the thorns of Jesus's crown, and the red berries with his blood.

In Celtic folklore, the Holly King ruled over the dark half of the year (from the summer solstice to winter solstice), and the Oak King ruled over the light half of the year (from the winter solstice to the summer solstice).

At the end of the year, a girl would dress in ivy (representing feminine forces) and a boy in holly (representing the masculine) in order to ensure fertility of crops for the new year ahead. Bringing holly inside was believed to protect the home from malevolent faeries and welcome in benevolent Fae. The ancient Romans would also decorate their homes with holly during Saturnalia on December 17 to celebrate the light during the darkest part of the year. This festival and its traditions were eventually incorporated into Christmas in Christian times.

MAGICKAL PROPERTIES

Holly protects against hexes and negative spirits. Hang holly above your front door to protect your home from negativity and dark magick, or carry a sprig of holly for personal protection. Add 4 tsp each of ground down holly leaves, dried agrimony, and nettle in 8.5 fl oz (250 ml) of carrier oil such as sunflower or jojoba oil and leave to infuse for 4–6 weeks, shaking daily. After this time, drain and discard the plant matter and use the oil to anoint the door of your home, yourself, or a piece of jewelry that you wear daily, to protect yourself from curses. This oil can be used to remove any negative magick that may have been placed upon you by using it to dress a black candle, letting the candle burn out, and thereby breaking the hex.

Holly is related to luck and fortune. Place some holly leaves in a bowl of water and leave it to infuse in the sunlight for 3–4 hours. Take out the leaves and use the water to spray yourself and your home to attract good luck into your life. The water can also be used for protective purposes.

MEDICINAL PROPERTIES

Holly leaves have calming and tranquilizing properties, and can be used to treat anxiety. Fill a tea ball infuser with 2 tsp each of holly leaves and holly-tree bark. Place it in hot water and leave to infuse for 15-20 minutes. Drink 2 cups a day for as long as the anxiety persists.

Holly leaves are an excellent diuretic and can relieve fluid retention. Make a decoction by adding 8 tbsp of both dried holly leaves and bark to 35 fl oz (1 liter) of hot water and boil for 15 minutes till they go mushy. Drain and discard the plant matter and drink 2–3 cups each day. This water can also be used to treat fevers.

DISCLAIMER:
Holly berries are poisonous to people and animals and should NEVER be consumed. The leaves are safe and non-toxic, but be aware of the spikey leaves of the holly tree, as they can cut and prick the skin.

ZODIAC SIGN
Cancer
♋

ELEMENT
Fire
△

PLANETS
Mars and Saturn
♂ ♄

HOLLY
Ilex aquifolium

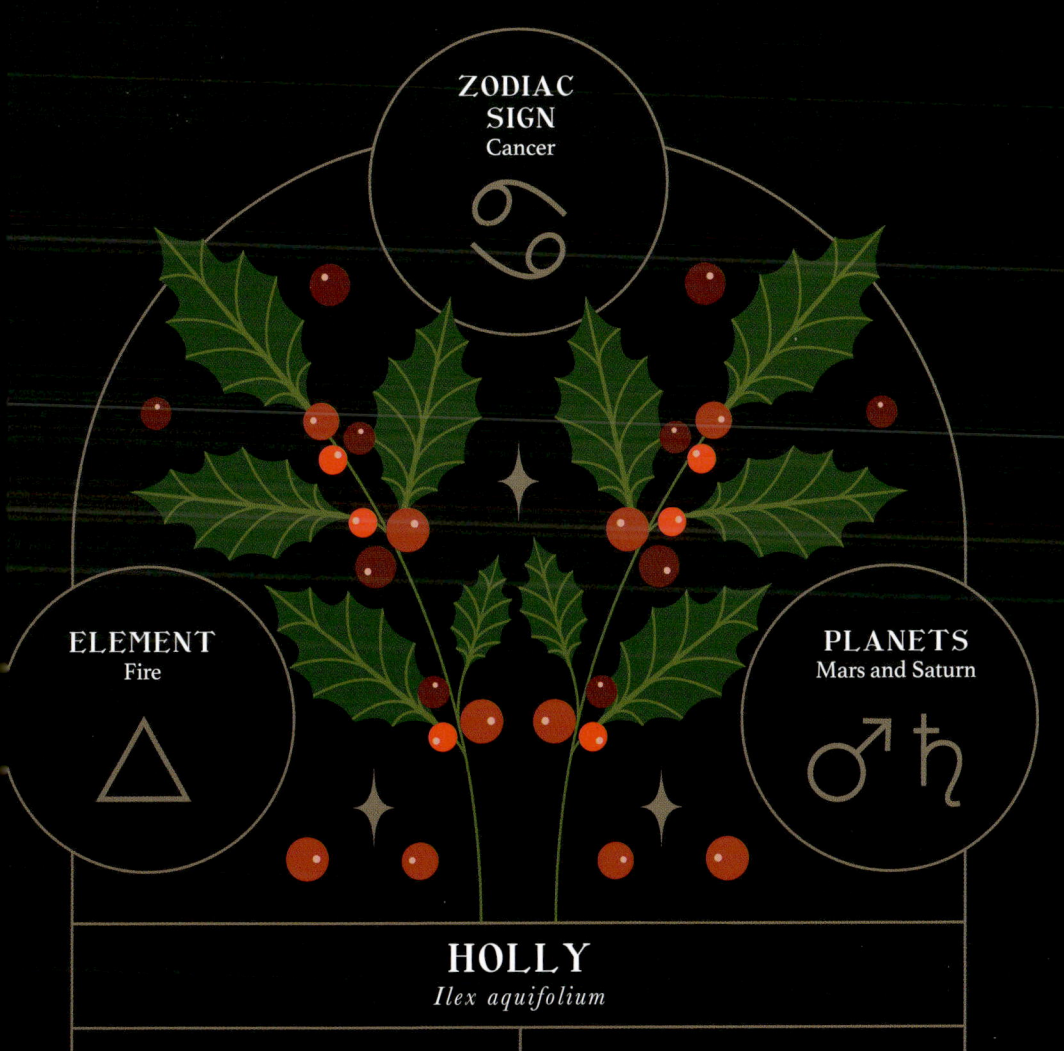

MAGICKAL PROPERTIES
- Protects against hexes and negative spirits
- Breaks hexes and curses
- Brings good luck, good fortune, and prosperity

MEDICINAL PROPERTIES
- Calms
- Promotes relaxation
- Treats anxiety
- Reduces fever
- Treats digestive issues

FOLK NAMES Aquifolius, Bat's Wings, Christ's Thorn, Holm Chase, Hulm, Hulver Bush, Tinne

OAK
Quercus robur

FOLKLORE

In Celtic folklore, the oak tree is associated with knowledge and wisdom. They were also believed to be the home of faeries, and the Irish and English saying "faerie folks are in old oaks" was a reminder to be careful of the Fae.

It is thought that the word Druid may derive from the Celtic word *doire*, meaning "knower of the oak tree," due to the tree's association with wisdom.

The Celts, the ancient Romans, and Greeks would wear oak leaves as a sign of high status. The Greeks associated this tree with Zeus, god of thunder, because of its ability to attract and survive lightning strikes. Similarly, in Norse mythology, the oak was associated with Thor, god of thunder, because it was understood that the tree would offer protection during a thunder and lightning storm.

MAGICKAL PROPERTIES

Oak trees are protective. Use the leaves to make an oil that you can use to anoint yourself and your home to ward off negative energy or harm, especially from evil and illness. Place 4 tsp of dried, ground-up oak leaves and 10 fl oz (300 ml) of carrier oil such as sunflower or jojoba oil in a jar and leave to infuse for 4 weeks in a cool, dark place, shaking daily. After this time, drain and discard the leaves and your oil is ready to use.

Acorns are associated with prosperity and abundance. Carry one in your pocket to attract these things into your life. If you are having problems conceiving, carry an acorn and give one to your partner to increase fertility and sexual potency.

Oak leaves can be used in a ritual bath. Use 1 tsp each of dried oak leaves, thyme, rosemary, and common garden sage in a hot bath to attract strength and wisdom, and for spiritual cleansing.

ZODIAC SIGN
Leo

ELEMENT
Fire

PLANETS
Jupiter and the Sun

OAK
Quercus robur

MAGICKAL PROPERTIES
- Brings protection, prosperity, and abundance
- Increases fertility and sexual potency
- Boosts strength and wisdom
- Cleanses spiritually

MEDICINAL PROPERTIES
- Treats muscle pain
- Treats eczema and cuts
- Good for oral health
- Aids digestive health

FOLK NAMES
Common Oak, Daur, English Oak, Pedunculate Oak, Royal Oak

MEDICINAL PROPERTIES

Oak leaves have anti-inflammatory properties. To reduce swelling and muscular pain, make an oak leaf salve and rub it onto the affected area. To make the salve, you will need 3 tsp of both dried oak leaves and green tea, 13.5 fl oz (400 ml) of olive oil, 4 drops of both lavender and eucalyptus essential oil, and 1 oz (30 g) of beeswax. Heat up the leaves, green tea, and oil in a double boiler for 15 minutes, then strain out the plant matter. Return to the stove and stir the beeswax into the infused oil until it's melted. Add the essential oils. While still hot, pour the liquid into an airtight jar and leave to harden before use. This salve can also be used to treat skin conditions like eczema, and to treat cuts.

Oak leaves are good for oral health. Place 3 tsp of leaves and 8.5 fl oz (250 ml) of vodka in a jar to make a tincture, leaving for 4 weeks before straining and discarding out the tree matter. The tincture can then be dabbed onto inflamed gums to reduce swelling. A decoction can also be made from oak bark to gargle with. Place 7 fl oz (200 ml) of water and 2 tsp of dried oak bark in a pan. Simmer for 20 minutes before draining away the bark, saving the water. Use twice a day. This water can also help digestive issues and as an astringent, can be used as a facial cleanser to tighten pores.

ROWAN
Sorbus aucuparia

FOLKLORE

In Celtic folklore, the rowan tree is associated with protection against Witchcraft. Rowan trees were often planted by the home to ward off negative energies, which was why it was considered bad luck to cut one down. The red berries of the rowan increased the tree's protective abilities, as red is traditionally seen as the best color to protect against magick.

In England, the rowan was commonly known as "the Witch tree," and its wood was often used to make protective talismans that were hung up with red thread around the home. The rowan was also the traditional wood used to make runes for divination.

The Celts associated rowan with Brigid, the goddess of healing, spinning, weaving, and smithing, and traditionally, spinning wheels were made from rowan wood in Ireland and Scotland. In Norse mythology, it was believed that a rowan tree saved Thor's life when he was swept away to the Underworld, but was able to grab a rowan branch to pull himself back.

MAGICKAL PROPERTIES

Rowan is associated with protection and banishing spells. Use a small piece of rowan wood to make a talisman with the rune Elhaz carved into it, which can be worn or carried to protect yourself against negative energies.

To protect your home, use rowan twigs and red string to make the shape of a pentacle, and hang it in your house. To protect yourself as you travel, thread dried rowan berries onto red string and wear as a necklace to keep you safe.

To banish a person or negative influences, write the thing you want to banish on a piece of paper and place it in a pouch filled with rowan leaves and berries, burying it in the ground somewhere far from your home and property. The early 16th-century Welsh Witch Tangwlyst ferch Glyn used a poppet filled with herbs, including rowan leaves, to banish (and curse) the Bishop of David when he accused her of living in sin.

MEDICINAL PROPERTIES

Rowan berries improve respiratory health. They reduce inflammation in the respiratory tract, soothe sore throats, and treat asthma. For these purposes, make a rowan berry syrup containing 5 tbsp of berries, 12 fl oz (350 ml) of water, and 5 tbsp of sugar. Simmer for 15 minutes before leaving to cool for 20 minutes. Use a potato masher to mash the berries to release as much juice as possible before discarding them. Although rowan berry seeds are safe to eat once cooked (they contain toxic parasorbic acid when uncooked) it's better to strain out the seeds using a cheesecloth, because it's not nice when you eat them and get them stuck in your teeth! Simmer the mixture until it turns into a syrup. Keep in an airtight jar in the refrigerator for up to a week, taking 1 tbsp, 3 times a day. This syrup can also help to boost immunity due to the high levels of vitamin C and can act as a digestive aid.

Rowan has anti-inflammatory and antimicrobial properties, and is used to relieve pain and treat and prevent infections. The syrup above can be taken 3 times a day for this purpose, or a berry juice can be made by simmering 5 tsp of rowan berries in 17 fl oz (500 ml) of water on a low heat until they are soft. Remove from the heat, mash the berries to release their liquid, and then strain and discard them. Drink 1 cup, 3 times a day, keeping in the refrigerator for up to 1 week.

DISCLAIMER:
Rowan berries are toxic when raw. Once cooked, they are safe to eat, so always cook them before consuming.

ZODIAC SIGN
Aquarius

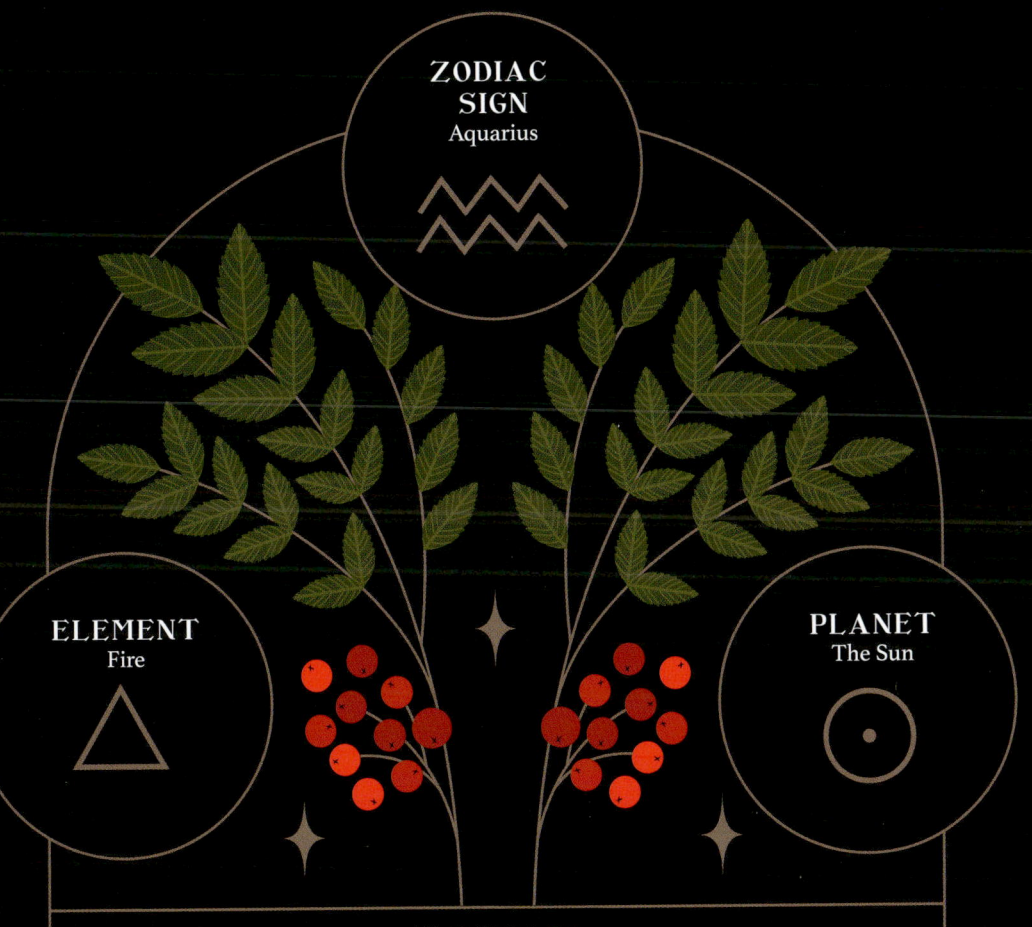

ELEMENT
Fire

PLANET
The Sun

ROWAN
Sorbus aucuparia

MAGICKAL PROPERTIES
- Protects and banishes
- Increases strength
- Brings mental clarity
- Increases psychic abilities
- Protect against bad luck
- Boosts resilience

MEDICINAL PROPERTIES
- Improves respiratory health
- Aids digestion
- Relieves pain
- Boosts immunity
- Improves appetite

FOLK NAMES Cuirn, Keirn, Mountain Ash, Rowan, Witch Wiggin Tree

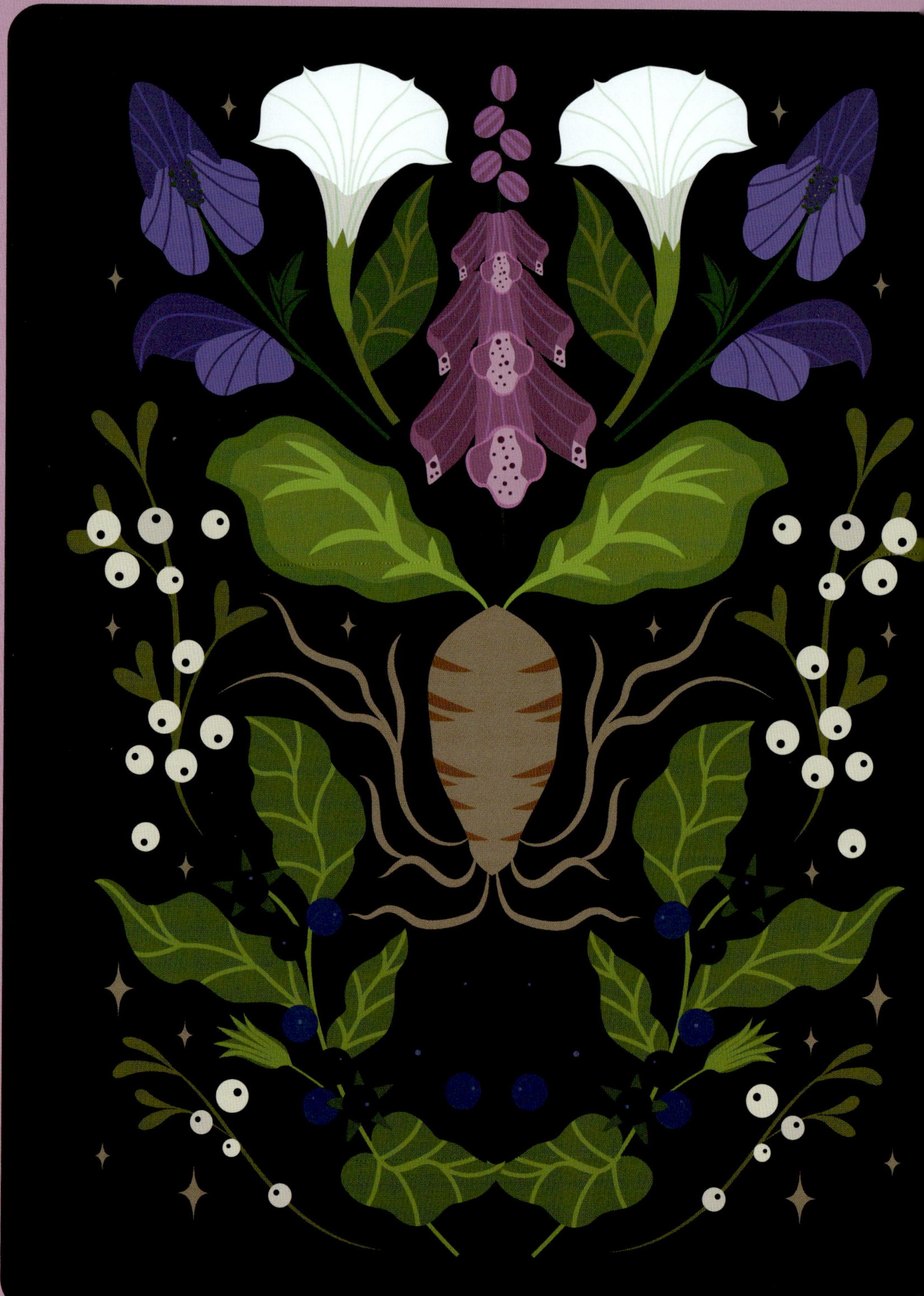

4
BANEFUL HERBS IN FOLKLORE

Baneful (or poisonous) herbs have been used for millennia both for their magickal and medicinal qualities. Even today, Witches and healers use baneful herbs in their practice. Many Witchcraft and herbal books do not include information about these kinds of herbs because they are so dangerous, and can easily kill a human being or animal if consumed. But as this book is about green folklore, I think it is important to include them because of the rich and colorful mythology attributed to poisonous herbs such as belladonna, foxglove, and mandrake. I will briefly touch on the magickal and medicinal properties of these plants purely for informational purposes, but my focus will be on their rich folklore and history.

DISCLAIMER:
It is of the utmost importance that you DO NOT consume or handle baneful herbs in any way, as even the smallest amounts can cause a great amount of pain and death. Even touching them without gloves can cause serious skin reactions, or even poisoning, as some of the toxins can enter the body through the skin. Some of these herbs may be prescribed by professionally trained medical herbalists, but are not safe to experiment with in any way.

BELLADONNA
Atropa belladonna

FOLKLORE & HISTORY

Known more commonly as deadly nightshade, belladonna is native to the UK, central and eastern Europe, and Asia, but has long since been naturalized in many other countries, including North America. Typically found in woods, thickets, waste ground, and on roadsides, it grows up to 4 ft (1.2 m) tall, and has mildly scented, purple bell-shaped flowers. It is one of the most toxic plants native to the Northern Hemisphere. The leaves, roots, and berries are extremely poisonous as they contain tropane alkaloids, which in small doses causes hallucinations and delirium, and in large doses will kill.

Meaning "beautiful lady" in Italian, folklore states that in the Renaissance period, Italian women often put a tincture of belladonna berries in their eyes, as they believed it would make them look more beautiful because it dilated their pupils. The name *Atropa* came from Atropos (meaning "the inflexible one"), one of the three Greek Fates, whose function was to render the decisions of her sisters irreversible and sever the thread of life.

In ancient Roman folklore, belladonna was sacred to Bellona, the goddess of war. Belladonna was used by the Romans to contaminate their enemies' food, and the wives of the Roman emperors Claudius and Augustus were poisoned by atropine, a toxic component found in belladonna. It was not just used as a weapon, but atropine was found to be the only antidote to a deadly, odorless gas created as a nerve agent by Nazi Germany in World War II.

In Bohemia, Belladonna was said to belong to the Devil, and anyone who ate the berries of the plant would be punished by him. Children were told they would meet the Devil face-to-face if they picked the berries. German folklore tells us that if you did want to pick the plant, you first had to release a black hen on Walpurgisnacht (May Eve), as the Devil would go and chase the animal and leave the belladonna unguarded.

In Europe, during the 16th and 17th centuries, belladonna was also a popular ingredient in flying ointment, which was a hallucinogenic ointment used by Witches to transport them to their Sabbat gatherings. You can find an alternative safe recipe for flying ointment on page 80.

Do Not Touch or Consume

ELEMENT
Water

PLANET
Saturn

BELLADONNA
Atropa belladonna

MAGICKAL PROPERTIES
- Aids astral projection
- Used in faery magick
- Protects

FOLK NAMES
Death Cherries, Banewort, Beautiful Death, Deadly Nightshade, Devil's Berries, Devil's Herb, Divale, Dwale, Dwayberry, Great Morel

DATURA
Datura stramonium

FOLKLORE & HISTORY

Commonly known as jimsonweed, datura is a bushy plant native to North America and Mexico. It is 12–24 in (30–60 cm) tall and has large trumpet-like flowers that produce a spiny fruit, which, when ripe, produces many seeds. Like belladonna, the leaves, roots, and flowers contain deadly tropane alkaloids, which can kill humans and animals even in small doses. Growing in places such as in fields, at roadsides, and in hedgerows, datura is often considered a weed.

In many indigenous cultures, datura was used as a shamanistic tool to aid divination and spirit work due to its mind-altering properties. Used for over 3,000 years, this visionary plant enabled access to the spirit world when smoked or used in an oil or ointment. In ancient Greece, the high priestess of the Temple of Apollo at Delphi, known as "the Delphi Oracle," also used datura by burning it and breathing in the smoke to help induce visions.

In European folklore, datura is often associated with the dark goddess Hecate. It's also connected to Baba Yaga, a crone who was a central figure in Slavic folklore and magick who was known for kidnapping and eating children. It was thought that datura was brought to other parts of Europe by the Roma when they migrated from the east, using it to invoke spirits. Often known as "Witches weed," Datura has a strong association with Witchcraft, magick, and the Underworld. It was a plant that was often used by Witches in flying ointments during the 16th and 17th centuries to enable Witches to travel to a Sabbat due to it's hallucinogenic properties (you can find a safe recipe for flying ointment on page 80.)

Datura is commonly used in India to decorate shrines, treat fevers, and reduce inflammation. However, it has a dark history. Followers of the goddess Kali used datura in criminal activity when they would drug their victims before stealing from them. Datura was also thought to be used to drug those chosen to be human sacrifices. The Aztecs used this plant as a narcotic to knock out their ritual sacrifices before removing their hearts.

Do Not Touch or Consume

ELEMENT
Water

PLANET
Saturn

DATURA
Datura stramonium

MAGICKAL PROPERTIES
- Helps find missing objects
- Breaks negative spells
- Protecs
- Inspires lust
- Increases psychic abilities
- Induces visions

FOLK NAMES
Thorn Apple, Devil's Snare, Devil's Trumpet, Jimsonweed

ELEMENT
Water

PLANET
Venus

FOXGLOVE
Digitalis purpurea

MAGICKAL PROPERTIES
- Protects
- Stops gossip
- Expels evil spirits
- Stops nightmares

FOLK NAMES
Cowflop, Dead Men's Bells, Fairy-Fingers, Fairybells, Fairy Herb, Fairy Petticoats, Fairyweed, Flapdock, Flop-a-Dock, Flop-Poppy, Flop-Top, Flopdock, Floppydock, Goblin Gloves, Gooseflops, Popdock, Rabbit's Flowers Thimbles, Witches Gloves

FOXGLOVE
Digitalis purpurea

FOLKLORE & HISTORY

The distinctive foxglove is native to Britain and western Europe. They can grow up to 60 in (150 cm) tall and have purple, yellow, and white bell-shaped flowers. They produce a fruit that yields many seeds, which change from green to black as they ripen. When not in flower, comfrey can be confused with foxglove, so beware when foraging for comfrey. Due to a poison called digitoxin, consuming foxglove causes vomiting, diarrhea, and death by damaging the heart and slowly decreasing the heartrate.

In European folklore, foxgloves were associated with faeries. In Britain, these flowers were originally known as "folk's gloves" in a reference to the faerie folk, and the dew collected from the flowers of this plant was also used in spells to communicate with the Fae. In England, it was considered unlucky to pick foxgloves, as faeries were believed to live in the bell-shaped flowers, and the little dots within the flowers itself were believed to be faerie footprints. It was believed that in order to stop the Fae from abducting a child, the juice of the foxglove was used to offer protection. Bringing them into the house was thought to be an invitation to the Devil to enter the home.

In Scandinavian folklore, it is said that foxes would wear the bell-shaped flowers of the foxglove around their necks, and that faeries taught them how to ring the bell in order to provide protection from hunters and their hounds. Foxes were also believed to use foxglove flowers on their paws so they could enter a chicken coop without being heard.

In ancient Rome, the foxglove was sacred to the goddess Flora, the goddess of women and childbirth, who made Hera pregnant by touching her stomach and breasts with the flowers of a foxglove.

Do Not Touch or Consume

HEMLOCK
Conium maculatum

FOLKLORE & HISTORY

Native to north west America but naturalized in Britain and Europe, hemlock is a highly poisonous plant that produces delicate white flowers in umbrella-like clusters. The leaves have a strong, unpleasant smell, and its stems are purple and spotted. Hemlock contains toxic alkaloids that work on the nervous system, and when consumed, even the smallest dose can depresses the respiratory system before causing death. Hemlock can be easily confused with yarrow, elderflower, and Queen Anne's lace to the untrained eye, so be very careful when foraging for these safe, nontoxic herbs, as even touching the leaves or flowers of hemlock can cause a skin reaction that feels and looks like a burn.

In European folklore, hemlock is known for its connection to Witches. In Britain, it is closely associated with Witchcraft and was a common way in which to murder others. In 16th-century Scottish folklore, the Witch and healer Agnes Sampson (also known as the Wise Wife of Keith) was accused at her trial of Witchcraft and of using hemlock to poison people in her village. In Shakespeare's play *Macbeth*, the brew that the three Witches concocted to conjure the souls of the dead contained root of hemlock, showing the supernatural associations of this plant during the 16th and 17th centuries. Due to its association with Witchcraft, this plant is also thought to be sacred to the Greek goddess Hecate.

In ancient Greece, it was customary for those being executed to choose their own method of death, and when the philosopher Socrates was to be executed after his trial, he chose hemlock tea. In ancient folklore, the enchantress Circe and the sorceress Medea are associated with this plant. Due to her vast knowledge of herbs, Circe would use the poisonous plant to kill and put spells upon men who would step onto her island, Aeaea. Medea, who fell in love with Jason, leader of the Argonauts, also used hemlock to murder her own two sons and Jason's daughter after Jason deserted her for the daughter of King Creon.

In folklore, the magickal properties of hemlock include protection, and it was used for consecration and for destructive charms.

Do Not Touch or Consume

ELEMENT
Water

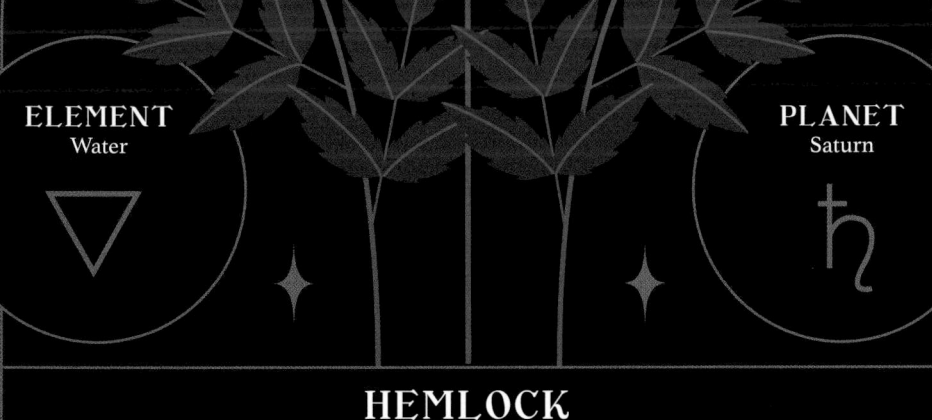

PLANET
Saturn

HEMLOCK
Conium maculatum

MAGICKAL PROPERTIES
- Purifies
- Honors Hecate
- Symbolizes immortality and rebirth

FOLK NAMES
Carrot Fern, Devil's Bread, Devil's Porridge, Poison Hemlock, Poison Parsley, Spotted Coroban

MANDRAKE
Mandragora officinarum

FOLKLORE & HISTORY

Mandrake is native to the southern Mediterranean and the Himalayas. The purple, blue, and violet clusters of its bell-shaped flowers have five petals, and orange colored fruit. When pulled out of the ground, the large roots are forked and can look like the form of a human with arms and legs. The roots, leaves, fruits, and flowers are toxic, and contain high levels of the tropane alkaloid, which will kill even in small doses. Initial symptoms after ingesting this plant include delirium and gastrointestinal distress, and after a while, the heartrate slows down before death occurs.

In folklore, mandrake, like belladonna and hemlock, had a strong association with magick. Along with these other plants, mandrake was frequently used by Witches in the Middle Ages as an ingredient in flying ointments. Witches were thought to travel to the Sabbats on their broomsticks when in reality, Witches used this as a type of hallucinogenic salve, which was applied to the skin for the purpose of soul flight and astral travel. The Italian Witch Matteuccia di Francesco, who used flying ointment for these purposes, claimed the perfect mixture to achieve the optimum effect contained mandrake, hemlock, opium, henbane, ivy, lapathum, lettuce, and the juice of an unripe mulberry. You can find a safe recipe for flying ointment on page 80.

According to folklore, when a mandrake plant was uprooted, it would scream loudly, killing anyone who heard the monstrous noise. It was believed that one extremely cruel way to uproot a mandrake without killing yourself was to cover your ears, tie the leash of a dog to a mandrake plant, back away, and then call the dog toward you. The dog would then run, uprooting the mandrake as it went, hear the scream, and die. The mandrake would then stop screaming, leaving you to take the plant unharmed.

Do Not Touch or Consume

ELEMENT
Fire

PLANET
Mercury

MANDRAKE
Mandragora officinarum

MAGICKAL PROPERTIES
- Purifies
- Protects
- Draws loved ones toward you

FOLK NAMES
Satan's Apple, Baaras, Circe's Plant, Circoeae, Devil's Testicle, Gallows, Manroot, Racoon Berry

ELEMENT
Air

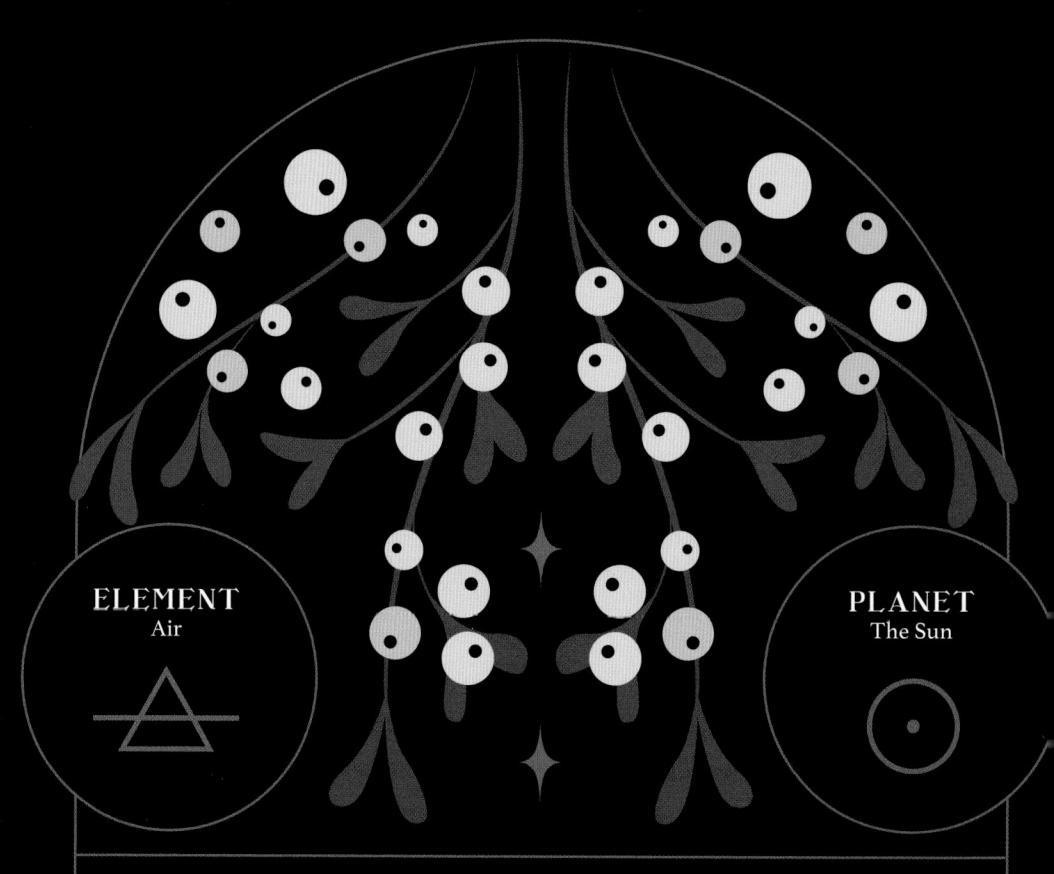

PLANET
The Sun

MISTLETOE
Viscum album

MAGICKAL PROPERTIES
- Love
- Fertility
- Vigor
- Empowerment
- Hope
- Good fortune
- Wealth

FOLK NAMES
Mislin Bush, Kiss and Go, Churchman's Greeting, All Heal, Devil's Five, Golden Bough, Witches' Broom, Wood of the Cross

MISTLETOE
Viscum album

FOLKLORE & HISTORY

Native to the Britain and most of Europe, mistletoe is a small evergreen plant with forked branches and clusters of white berries. It's known as a parasitic shrub, because it grows around other trees such as hawthorn, poplar, and apple trees, taking water and nutrients from them to survive. While it doesn't kill the trees it grows around, it can weaken them substantially. While mistletoe doesn't kill when ingested, the toxic proteins called phoratoxin and viscotoxin cause nausea and vomiting if eaten.

In Norse folklore, mistletoe was the only thing that could kill Odin's son Baldur, god of light, wisdom, and courage. Baldur suffered nightmares about his death, so his mother Frigg made everything in the natural world, including animals and plants, swear an oath that they would not harm him. Loki, god of mischief, found some mistletoe, which was too small and young to make the promise to Frigg that it would not hurt Baldur. Loki gave some mistletoe to his brother, Hodr, who, not understanding what he was doing, threw the mistletoe at Baldur, killing him. In one version of the story, Frigg was so distraught that she declared she would never hurt another living thing, and instead would work to bring love into the world, and proclaimed she would kiss anyone that stood under the mistletoe. In a happier version, Baldur was resurrected by the gods and Frigg was so overjoyed that she declared mistletoe a symbol of love, promising to kiss anyone who stood beneath it.

In European folklore, mistletoe is probably best known for its association with kissing under its boughs at Christmas. In the 1700s, it became a part of Christmas tradition for men to steal a kiss from any woman who stood beneath a sprig of mistletoe. To refuse would bring bad luck.

Druids believed that mistletoe was sacred, but it was most sacred of all when it was growing from an oak tree. When the oak tree lost its leaves in the fall, the Druids believed that the spirit of the tree passed into the green mistletoe for the winter until its return in spring. The Celts used mistletoe as a protection charm to ward off evil spirits, and it was hung above the front door to ensure negative spirits couldn't enter.

Do Not Touch or Consume

MONKSHOOD
Aconitum napellus

FOLKLORE & HISTORY

Monkshood is native to Europe and Britain, but has been naturalized in countries across the Northern Hemisphere. Also known as wolfsbane, monkshood has distinctive clusters of hooded purply-blue flowers, dark green leaves, and erect finger-like green pods containing thousands of seeds. The flowers, leaves, roots, and seeds are highly toxic, containing alkaloids such as aconitine. In lower doses, these chemicals cause gastrointestinal issues, chest pain, and numbness and tingling throughout the body. In larger doses, it depresses the respiratory system and changes the rhythm of the heart before causing death.

According to ancient Greek mythology, monkshood was formed from the saliva of the three-headed dog of Hades, called Cerberus, who guarded the gates of Hell. It grew wherever the saliva fell onto the ground, giving it the name wolfsbane. Monkshood was also associated with Theseus, a great hero in Greek mythology, and his father King Aegeus. Medea, wife of Aegeus, tried to poison Theseus with an infusion of wine and monkshood, but when Aegeas saw the sword Theseus was carrying and realized it was his son, he grabbed the cup and threw it to the floor.

In ancient Rome, monkshood was associated with murder. The Roman naturalist Pliny the Elder wrote about how Lucius Calpurnius Bestia, a senator, smeared monkshood root onto his finger and touched the genitalia of his sleeping wife, killing her. As a consequence, Pliny then gave the plant the name *thelyphonon*, meaning "lady killer."

In Anglo-Saxon times, monkshood root was used to cover the tips of arrows when hunting wolves, which led to it being named wolfsbane. Monkshood was also thought to ward off and even to cure the bite of a werewolf.

Monkshood has a long association with Witchcraft. It is the most poisonous plant to be found in Britain, yet despite this, like many other baneful herbs, it was still included in Witch's flying ointment. You can find a safe recipe for flying ointment on page 80.

In Nordic folklore, this plant was associated with Thor, the god of thunder, and was known as Thor's hat. It was also believed to be sacred to Thor's father Odin, god of war and death, and Hel, the goddess and death and the Underworld.

Do Not Touch or Consume

ELEMENT
Water

PLANET
Saturn

MONKSHOOD
Aconitum napellus

MAGICKAL PROPERTIES
- Protects
- Boosts courage and strength
- Sacred to the goddess Hecate

FOLK NAMES
Blue Rocket, Conite, Devil's Hat, Devil's Helmet, Helmet Flower, Leopard's Bane, Monkshood, Queen of Poisons, Wolfsbane, Woman's Bane

CONCLUSION

Folklore is knowledge, beliefs or practices that have been passed down from one generation to another simply by word of mouth, and there are so many stories associated with herbs, flowers, trees, and plants. It's incredible how much of this folklore has survived the hundreds and sometimes thousands of years, and now that much of this folklore has been written down, it's recorded for posterity and won't be lost to the sands of time.

This folklore can enrich our Witchcraft practice as we can understand more about the magickal and medicinal properties of these green ingredients and, therefore, how we can use them today in our Craft, both in spells and in healing practices. I truly hope the stories in this book have not only inspired you but the knowledge contained within them will help you as you practice the Craft both now and in years to come.

CITED WORKS

Margaret Baker, *Discovering the Folklore of Plants* (Boxley, 1969)

Rebecca Beyer, *Wild Witchcraft* (Simon Element, 2022)

Paul Beyerl, *The Master Book of Herbalism* (Phoenix Publishing, 1984)

Corinne Boyer, *The Witch's Cabinet* (Three Hands Press, 2021)

Marcel De Cleene, Marie Claire Lejune, *Compendium of Symbolic and Ritual Plants in Europe, Volumes 1 and 2* (Man & Culture Publishers, 2003)

Scott Cunningham, *Encyclopedia of Magical Herbs* (Llewellyn Publications, 1985)

Cora Linn Daniels, C. M. Stevans, *Encyclopaedia of Superstitions, Folklore & The Occult Sciences of the World: Volume 2* (University Press of the Pacific, 2003)

Ronald M. Davidson, *Indian Esoteric Buddhism* (Columbia University Press, 2002)

S. Theresa Dietz, *The Complete Language of Flowers* (Wellfleet Press, 2022)

James A. Duke, *Handbook of Medicinal Herbs* (CRC Press, 1985)

Gemma Gary, *Traditional Witchcraft* (Troy Books, 2011)

John Gerard, *Gerard's Herbal* (Random House, 1994)

Jacob Grimm, Wilhelm Grimm, Jacob Browning, *The Pied Piper of Hamelin* (George G. Harrap & Co, 1842)

Gabrielle Hatfield, *Encyclopedia of Folk Medicine* (ABC-CLIO, 2004)

R.M. Heanly, *Folklore* (Forgotten Books, 1911)

Fez Inkwright, *Folk Magick and Healing* (Liminal 11, 2019)

James George Frazer, *The Golden Bough: Volume II* (Outlook Verlag, 2020)

Paul Kendall, *Mythology & Folklore of Elder Trees* (Trees for Life, 2020)

Sandra Lawrence, *Witch's Garden* (Welbeck Publishing, 2020)

Coby Michael, *The Poison Path Herbal* (Park Street Press, 2021)

R.C. Parker, "Psychoactive Plants in Tantric Buddhism." *Erowid Extracts*, June 2008, pp. 6-11. https://erowid.org/spirit/traditions/buddhism/buddhism_tantra_article1.shtml

Nigel G. Pearson, *Wortcunning* (Troy Books, 2019)

Christian Rätsch, *The Encyclopedia of Psychoactive Plants* (Park Street Press, 2005)

Sarah Robinson, *Kitchen Witch* (Womancraft Publishing, 2022)

FURTHER READING

Gary Allen, *Herbs: A Global History* (Edible), (Reaktion Books, 2012)

Tom Atkinson, *Napiers History of Herbal Healing Book, Ancient and Modern* (Napiers, 2008)

Michael Brown, *Death in the Garden: Poisonous Plants and Their Use Throughout History* (White Owl, 2018)

Nicholas Culpeper, (edited by Raven StarHawk Cunningham), *Culpeper's Complete Herbal* (CreateSpace Independent Publishing Platform, 2008)

Gemma Garry, *Silent as the Trees: Devonshire Witchcraft, Folklore & Magick,* (Troy Books, 2017)

Jesse Wolf Hardin, *Folk Herbalist: Traditional Practice, Plant Folklore, Kitchen Medicine, & Community Herbalism* (Independently published, 2020)

Fez Inkwright, *Botanical Curses and Poisons: The Shadow Lives of Plants* (Liminal 11, 2021)

Sandra Lawrence, *Witch's Forest: Trees in magic, folklore and traditional remedies* (Welbeck, 2023)

Angela Paine, *Healing Plants of Greek Myth* (John Hunt Publishing, 2022)

Richard Evans Schultes, Albert Hofmann, Christian Rätsch, *Plants of the Gods: Their Sacred, Healing, and Hallucinogenic Powers* (Healing Arts Press, 2001)

Richard Le Strange, *A History of Herbal Plants* (Angus and Robertson, 1977)

Jane Wilde, *Folk Medicine, Plant Lore, and Healing Plants* (Pierides Press, 2019)

Margaret Willes, *A Shakespearean Botanical* (The Bodleian Library, 2015)